HARPER-ARRINGTON
P U B L I S H I N G

The Official Step-by-Step Guide to Starting a Clothing Line - Edition 4.2

ISBN: 0976416107

Special Notice: If you purchased this book and the cover is missing or the cover does not match the one on our website, or it has markings made my someone else – please contact us immediately at 888-435-9235. If you believe that this book appears to a photocopied book – contact us as well!

Harper-Arrington Publishing LLC
33228 W 12 Mile Rd. Suite 105
Farmington Hills, MI 48334
T: 888-435-9234
F: 248-281-0373
Website: www.StartingaClothingLine.com and DigitalFashionPro.com
Email: support@startingaclothingline.com

Edited By Marc D. Baldwin, PhD

Printed in the United States of America

Disclaimer:
This book is for your general reference on starting a clothing line. We have taken every step to ensure that all the information presented here is accurate. We are not lawyers and therefore we are not contending to give you any legal advice. We give you suggestions to follow at your own will. We cannot be held liable for any of the information presented in this book. You are completely responsible for any decisions that you make.

Titles currently available from Harper Arrington:

Please note that all three of our guides work together to make up our full course on starting your own clothing line and being successful at running it. We also have a contact list with over 400 great fashion industry suppliers including manufacturers, button makers and more on our web site.

Digital Fashion Pro – The Ultimate Fashion Design Software – The premiere design tool for apparel designers. Create hot designs, spec sheets, catalogs and more right on your computer with ease with this revolutionary design kit.

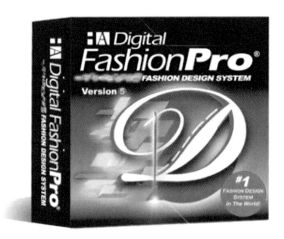

All these resources and more are available at:

DigitalFashionPro.com / StartingaClothingLine.com

TABLE OF CONTENTS

Chapter I – Starting Your Line

Chapter II – The Reality of Owning Your Own Line

Chapter III – How to Effectively Sell Your Line to Retailers

INTRODUCTION TO CHAPTER I

This guide was written to inform aspiring designers how to start and officially launch their own clothing line. The clothing industry is a ninety billion dollar per year industry that is constantly growing. It is our intention through this guide to give you a down to earth, comprehensive look at what you will need to get going and stay going in the clothing design business. Whether you want to design leather, denim, urban, contemporary, or skateboard wear, our guide will put you on the right track.

The few books on this subject are written by authors who are not in touch with what is going on in today's marketplace. They do not have the experience in starting a clothing line from scratch. Our brand is an upscale urban brand started in late 1999 that has made contributions to the fashion industry by introducing innovative garments. Our experience is so great that we know for a fact that no other author can deliver the information to you like we can. We are fully credible and proficient to inform you on how to start your own line.

We did not release our first collection until March of 2002. It took us almost three years, and even up to now, to learn everything that we are putting here at your fingertips. We have worked with various manufacturers from all over the world. Our clothing is sold in boutiques across the U.S. and in Japan. Our clothing has been featured in movies, television shows and videos. We have been featured in various magazines like *XXL*, *Honey*, *The Stuff*, and *Rolling Out*, as well as in local magazines in different cities.

Some of the key points you will learn in this guide include:

- A step-by-step walk through the information that will get you going
- Money saving tips ✓
- Learn how to create your own trademarks (save on lawyer fees) ✓
- What makes a good brand name
- How to incorporate your business and why you should
- Learn about letter of credit for production / payment on TT ✓
- How to reduce the time it takes to get your line going ✓
- Valuable resources and contacts at your fingertips
- Learn about Production and Distribution Deals
- Getting a sales tax license
- Creating your website
- RN # issued from the government and why you need it ✓
- How to build the right team behind you
- How to find and deal with overseas manufacturers
- Getting orders at the famous Magic Tradeshow and other forums
- Go from being a T-shirt Designer to a real brand
- Designing your collection / specifications
- Style forecasting
- Managing cash flow ✓
- What is factoring and how to get it?
- Advertising and Marketing your brand
- Financing your line ✓
- How to go about doing photo shoots

- How and where to find models

- Importing, Visas and Custom House Brokers

- Quota System and Duties

- Distribution and getting your product in stores

- Keystoning and setting the right price for your products

- Packaging your products

- Key office points, taxes and accounting

- Valuable advice from the authors

- Inside industry secrets and much more

- Update to this 4th Edition: New way to pay manufacturers safely!

- How to Effectively Sell Your Line to Retailers and More!

ABOUT THE AUTHORS

The two authors of this guide are leading young designers currently operating and designing a national clothing line. The authors have been fortunate to experience firsthand the key points of the clothing industry. They know what it is like to start a line from scratch and actually move that product into stores. The authors have had some of their pieces worn by several celebrity figures. They have been truly dedicated to the fashion industry since their entry. Their passion for designing has been felt by customers all around the world. You are learning from two of the best.

Words from Michael H. on Chapter I

I wanted to write this guide to help people understand what it will take to make their dreams of becoming a fashion designer come true. The clothing business is not one of the easiest businesses to go into, especially if uninformed. Many people see a celebrity wearing a certain line or think that a sweet logo and a name is all it takes to be successful.

Our experiences are lessons to learn from. I became really aware of what we had to offer when I visited a design school a few months ago. We were looking for interns and we had to meet with the faculty as the first step to getting them.

Members of the faculty were really excited about the real world experience that we could bring to their students. I also found from my research of other publications on this subject that most writers lack the real world experience of what starting a clothing line is actually like. Volume I and II of this book will put the knowledge and insight at your fingertips. What you do with it is entirely up to you.

Words from Jay Arrington on Chapter I

The guide that you hold in your hands offers potential power for the fashion entrepreneur, but what you do with it will determine the outcome of your empowerment. At your fingertips is a long and rough road of experience; fortunately for you a large portion of that road has been eliminated. So what I would like to share with you is my understanding of the law of success. I truly hope that these words will stick with you on your journey to becoming the next hot designer.

Okay, once you have read and gained understanding of this guide, you are ready to take the walk of fame. On this walk, one simple rule applies in order for you to become successful. That rule is to never stop walking. As long as you continue to walk towards success – and success, after all, is the universal law of nature – eventually you will get there. There are three laws you must conquer on your journey to success: desire, opposition, and overcoming opposition. When you desire, the universe sets a test to see if you truly want what you desire. It does this by placing opposition in front of you. This opposition prepares you to be able to maintain what it is you desire by molding you into the person you need to become. Your continuous walk towards success regardless of any obstacle will enforce the third law: overcoming opposition. This will prove that you truly wanted what you desired and set out to achieve.

So remember. The first law is desire, the second law is opposition, and the third law, which is most important, is overcoming opposition. The third law is where you and your team must shine. So keep walking and you will achieve success at becoming the next hot designer.

Choosing a name is one of the most important things you will do in getting your clothing line started. Why is this important? Your name will affect the way you are viewed by others as well as where your clothing can and cannot go. For example, suppose you name your line something like Ghetto Moon. Yes, this is an urban name and it is okay if that is your market from here until the end.

You could do jeans, t-shirts or hats with this name, no problem. What if you wanted to do dress clothes under the brand name Ghetto Moon? Would it work? When picking your name, come up with something clever, unique and solid. Pick a name that represents what you want to do in the short term and in the long run. Pick a name that will excite and motivate you and others.

Brand Name, Company Name and Choosing Your Business Type

Your brand name and company name can be different, and really should be. For instance, your company could be your initials, while your line is called Ghetto Moon. Next, you will need to choose your business type. You could either register as a **DBA** with your local city government or incorporate as a **Limited Liability Company** (LLC). If you choose to become a DBA, you still will want to get your federal tax ID number from the federal government. **Call 1-800-829-1040**. Your federal tax ID number may still end up being your social security number unless you have partners. LLC is the best way to go as it will offer you more legal protection. The best place to seek incorporating services is on the Internet. Services found on the Internet tend to be cheaper than services rendered through a local attorney. ████████████████████

████████████████████████

Note: We are not attorneys and therefore are not giving you legal advice. If you have any questions or confusion, do not hesitate to contact a lawyer. Be sure to understand all of the benefits and drawbacks to each method of choosing your business type. If you incorporate, the government will issue you a **Tax Identification Number** as well.

Next, you must do a search to make sure no one else has any claims to your brand name or names that you are considering. Many people hire lawyers to do this, but keep in mind it will cost you. Our advice is to do your own search using the **United States Trademark System online**. Note, however, that just because you do not find anyone using your chosen name does not mean that it is completely clear.

Only an attorney can do a complete search. The catch is that if your name is unique and it does not come up in the search, then more than likely it is free and clear. **Attorney fees** for the entire process plus the filing fees could run you $850 on up. As I said, it is possible for you to do this without a lawyer.

Another way to search for the possible usage of your name by others is to visit the United States Patent and Trademark's online office at:

- http://tess2.uspto.gov/bin/gate.exe?f=searchss&state=i4p45h.1.1
- http://www.uspto.gov/main/trademarks.htm
- http://www.uspto.gov

The current cost to do a trademark electronically through the government's site is $335. When at the trademark website, have your credit card ready. Once again, we are not giving you legal advice. But the class at which most clothing companies start is **Class 25**. Class 25 can cover items such as:

Men's, women's and children's clothing, namely, t-shirts, pants, shirts, coats, sweatshirts, suits, knit shirts, jeans, dress shirts, vests, sweaters, shorts, swimwear, jackets, rainwear, blouses, dresses, sox, hosiery, underwear, footwear, pajamas, sleepwear, boxer shorts and women's lingerie and fashion accessories, namely, belts, leather gloves, scarves, hats, head bands, bandannas and neck ties.

For every **category or class of goods** you apply for, you will be **charged $335**. You will have to register your brand name as a trademark as well as any additional logo if the brand name and logos are separate in the category(s) you choose. Trademarks give you sole right to use the name. Side note: After registering, you will receive countless mail from attorney offices offering to watchdog your trademark in case someone else tries to use it. You also will receive mail from attorneys offering to register your trademark in foreign countries because you have no protection outside of the United States. Utilize these services if you want and can afford them. Make sure you fully investigate them, as scams are rampant.

After checking the availability of your brand name, it is time to create your logo. Make sure you really like the logo you create before you register it. If you or someone you know cannot make your logo, you can hire talent from logo creation services. Keep in mind the following example when figuring out the cost of doing your trademark.

RocaWear clothing company uses RW and Rocawear as its trademarks. The company has two separate trademarks in category 25, which costs a total of $670.

Moreover, if you have a favorite slogan that you would like to attach to your brand, it will have to be trademarked in same way that your name is. For example, say your slogan is "our fit is like a glove." You will have to trademark this. The slogan cannot be copyrighted as some think. We wish it could, as copyrights only cost about $30.

Next you should apply for a **sales tax license** through your local state government. This is important if you plan to sell directly to customers as well. If you will not be selling directly to the public, then you do not need a sales tax license. Hint: If you are only going to work wholesale, make sure your state government knows this. Otherwise, it will seek to charge you a use tax. A use tax is tax on the value of your imports and it says that you are using the imported goods for personal use. When the state knows you are just a wholesaler, they will not charge you anything.

Next you will need an **RN** # to import goods into the United States. Exercise: Look at some of the clothing you have around your house. Look at the woven labels in the inside and you are bound to see some RN numbers. Every importer of clothing must use them. Issuing an RN number is the government's way of identifying a company as an importer. You will give your RN number to your manufacturer upfront to document. The good news is that RN numbers are free. To get your RN number, visit the Federal Trade Commission at:

- http://www.ftc.gov/
- http://www.ftc.gov/bcp/rn/index.html

The next step is locking down a **website under your brand name**. Do a domain search for your brand name. Hopefully it is free and clear. Next, register it. One of the cheapest websites that we have seen register domain names is **godaddy.com.** Domain names cost about $14.95 per year at this site. You can create a website yourself by using resources like Wordpress, Shopify or 3dCart. If you do not have the time or skill to create a website, you can always hire a web designer.

Our Services:

If you want help with designing your line, creating tech packs, creating artwork, logos, prints or need direct consulting we can help – Visit: https://startmyline.com/consulting-services/

GETTING YOUR OFFICE / BUSINESS TOGETHER

Once you have registered your name, received your numbers, and signed up to pay taxes, it is time to get your office together. We recommend starting out in your home unless you have some significant money behind you already. You will need to create professional business cards, letter head, and envelopes. These things will display your company image.

Make sure you have your Internet connection together. Make sure you have a good printer, fax machine and other office essentials as well. Now, if you do not want to rent two phone lines or have your faxes coming through your business line, a good alternative is to use an online fax service. You will find it cheaper than getting a second line. Faxes are delivered to you via your email address. See http://startingaclothingline.com/html/**fashionbusinesslinks**.html for detailed information on fax services.

Next you will want to set up a bank account in the business name. Be sure to pay attention to bank fees and other regulations when deciding on a bank. Make sure they issue you credit and debit cards in the business name.

Next you will want to set up a shipping account with companies like USPS, FedEX or United Parcel Service (UPS).

FedEx: 800-463-3339 or visit fedex.com

Ups: 800-742-5877 or visit ups.com

For Fed Ex or UPS to work, you will need to get a mailing address! This could be your office if you have one outside of your home. If you have a home office, then you will want to set up a mail box with a local UPS Store. You may want to avoid post office boxes. They do not portray a professional look nor will Fed Ex or UPS deliver to them.

The cost for a UPS mailbox may be around $20 to $50 per month, depending on your box size. Once you have an account, the UPS store where your mailbox is located will accept your packages for free.

Next, make sure you have accounting software or programs like Microsoft Excel spread sheets to keep track of all of your expenses.

Creating Your Business Plan

1. Every business needs a plan. If you haven't already, formulate a business plan. The business plan is the blueprint of your clothing business. In this guide, we will not go too much into how to write a business plan, as there are plenty of books on this subject. You can also go to your local SBA office for help in writing your business plan. Some of the things you will include in the plan are your mission statement, products you want to manufacture, projections, a marketing plan, and everything in-between. The basic business plan outline is as follows:

   - **Executive Summary**: Write this last. It is just a page or two of highlights.

   - **Company Description**: Describe the company's legal establishment, history, and start-up plans, among other things.

   - **Product or Service**: Describe what you are selling. Focus on customer benefits.

   - **Market Analysis**: You need to know your market, customer needs, where they are, how to reach them, and so on.

   - **Strategy and Implementation**: Be specific. Include management responsibilities with dates and budgets. Make sure you can track results.

   - **Web Plan Summary**: For e-commerce, include discussion of your website, development costs, operations, sales and marketing strategies.

   - **Management Team**: Describe the organization and the key management team members.

   - **Financial Analysis**: Make sure to include, at the very least, your projected Profit and Loss and Cash Flow tables.

Note: You might want to wait and write your plan after reading our guides. This will help make your plan the best that it can be.

Designing is the fun part of the clothing business. Unfortunately for the designer or entrepreneur, designing per se only represents about 10-15% of what you will be doing overall. Nevertheless, it is definitely exciting when you see your ideas jump off the paper into real life. We still love it. Now if all you want to do is design, then you should be prepared to hire a lot of people to do all of the other duties involved in starting a clothing line.

Another piece of advice is to keep your initial offering simple in scope. Do not try to do too much too fast. Why should you keep it simple? Russell Simmons once said to me that the best thing to do is specialize in one thing. Make it big with that one thing, and then branch out into other areas and categories. This is the best and least expensive way. You cannot go wrong with this approach. This strategy allows you to become an expert and makes you that much more effective in many ways, ranging from cost to marketing to quality.

How can you narrow down what you offer? After all, like any entrepreneur, you probably have hundreds of ideas. Here are some helpful hints. First, you should make a choice to do men's, women's or children's apparel. This is your most important decision in this context. Do not try to do all of these categories at once. Do not let outside influences, such as customers, family or friends, talk you into doing more than one category when you begin. It is very expensive to produce more than one line in the initial stages of a clothing company. You would need a very substantial amount of capital to pull this off. At the same time, if your funds are limited, you will not be able to put out a good representation (for example, the amount of different styles you offer per season) of each line.

Just starting off, you can take things slowly. You may just want to begin by making T-shirts or even hats – just to get your feet wet. Possible places to buy blank T's and hats are:

- Broder Brothers (blanks): 1-800-543-4200
- American Apparel: http://www.americanapparel.net
- Promotional Headwear: 1-800-221-4744
- http://shop.startingaclothingline.com

██

████████ We also have the **Ultimate List** which features over 400 fashion industry suppliers and manufacturers. Each list can be found on our website.

You will need your sales tax number or tax identification number to buy T-shirts from these companies at wholesale prices. Make sure you have it. Call these places for a catalog.

The next step after getting your blank items in is to add your design to them. A domestic made T-shirt is great for sales and promotions. Look through your local yellow pages or search online for screen printers and embroidery shops. Now, while you may think domestic sourcing in this area is more expensive than overseas, it really is not. They are around the same price depending on the quantities you order, and they are a lot faster to get.

Unless you are designing 3,000 plus T-shirts, overseas manufacturing will be expensive. The main reason people want T-shirts made overseas instead of at home is because those made overseas can have special labels sewn into them. We are here to tell you that you could also have your own labels sewn into your blanks domestically.

The next phase in designing is to create your collection. You must have a **niche** to be successful. Your products must fill a current void in the market. You must be different but hot at the same time. Anybody can be different; it is not hard to do. Being different and hot at the same time is the thing to be. What will make your line stand out besides your name and logo?

Design your collection around seasons. You have to create based on the delivery dates per season. In general, the seasons are as follows:

- Fall Delivery: July – September
- Winter Delivery: September – December
- Spring Delivery: January – March
- Summer Delivery: April – June

There are a few things to keep in mind about delivery dates. The first thing is that most of the department stores buy at least two seasons in advance. So, say it is January 1, 2019. Your larger department stores, like Macy's, are buying anywhere from Fall '19, Winter '19, to Spring '20. Your smaller stores and boutiques usually buy one to two seasons in advance, but will buy your immediate delivery items as well.

The next thing is lining up your fabrications and styles to be used in each season's collection. Keep in mind delivery dates. For example, receiving an order of shorts in the month of June is not good. Why? You only have June and July to sell them. Stores do not want to take any deliveries of shorts after June. At this point, they are preparing to put their fall items out. The other thing to consider is that you are using the appropriate weight of fabric for the season.

During your style forecasting, you should always be concerned when the items you are designing are coming out. This will save you a lot of money and stress. You really want to make sure you are ahead or right on time with the season. Factors that determine this will be covered in later sections of this guide.

We will not go into a lot on designing, as there are plenty of books available on this subject.

Design Schools

There are various fashion design schools available. Going to school for design is a good idea. For those of you who are not in school or planning to go, do not be too upset. It is possible to start a clothing line without going to school. The more you know about every aspect of this industry, the greater your success will be. We repeat this throughout our book. It is an essential truth. Knowing your business inside and out will also save you money because you do not have to pay others to do things that you can do. In the end, whether you learn from books, going to school, or a combination of both, the main thing is to apply yourself. Learn all you can. If you choose the school route, check your local yellow pages to find fashion design schools in your area.

Sewing

It is possible to start your own line of clothing without knowing how to sew. It is a great benefit if you do sew, however, for a number of reasons. You can save money on creating samples if you sew them yourself. You will have a better insight on garment construction that will help you in various matters of quality when dealing with manufacturers. Once again, you should seek to learn all you can, and that includes learning how to sew. To find sewing classes, just look in your local yellow pages or go to fabric stores in your area which will most likely have flyers from people offering sewing lessons.

If you already know how to sew and create your own patterns, great! You have one advantage already. You can also find and work with a local seamstress if you can't sew. The best place to find a seamstress is by going through your local yellow pages, hanging out at fabric stores, or placing a classified ad in your local newspaper. You will get a response. These are the methods we used to find our first seamstress.

Choosing Your Fabrications

Coming up with the right fabrication for your styles is fun. You should do some trend analysis to see what your market is doing. You could take some trips to your local malls to see what other designers are doing as well. You could either choose to do something different from what is out or you could take the safe route and use fabrics currently in style.

Make sure you also consider the fabric's quality and traits before choosing it. A trip to your local fabric store is in order. There you will be able to purchase a few yards of fabric for sampling and swatches. Fabric is also available over the Internet.

Another thing to consider during designing is choosing your colors for the season. You could follow the trend or go against it. Both will have their rewards as long as the colors are hot. The official book on identifying colors is the **Pantone Textile Color Guide**. This is the international standard of color. Each color is defined by a pantone number. This number can be given to your overseas manufacturer to help her define the colors you want in your styles. You will definitely need this book. This fabulous book is available on our website.

If the fabric stores in your city do not have great fabrics like some of the things you see in your market, you will have to buy other designer's offerings and cut them up for swatch reference. This is an expensive practice but may be necessary to get as close to the fabric you want to use when you have limited resources. Not all of us live in New York City or L.A.

The next thing to do if you have not done so is to make your sketches or computer illustrated drawings. We have to say that computer aided designing, using programs like Digital Fashion Pro or Adobe Illustrator is the best way to design. Hand drawn sketches are cool too, but manufacturers don't really like them. One fantastic fashion design tool is our program Digital Fashion Pro formerly Harper Arrington Digital Design System. DF-Pro offers you the ability to make the most realistic looking computerized sketches using our trademarked Digital Fabric and Garment Templates.

DF-Pro can also be used to design technical sketches, catalogs, line sheets and more. Visit our website to learn more about this fabulous design system (DigitalFashionPro.com).

At this point you have your sketch. Now you will need to know about measurements. We actually teach you how to set up your technical sketches and spec sheets in a tutorial located on our Digital Fabric Library – Upgrade.

Specifications Sheet

Many new designers who have not gone to school or have studied specs on their own try to take the easy route. They simply buy and give another designer's clothes (do not confuse this with cutting up something for fabric swatch reference) to the seamstress or manufacturer and tell him or her to "make the fit just like these." This is a bad practice.

It is also an illegal practice. Measurements belong to that company for that garment and you are stealing if you do this.

- This is a very lazy approach to designing. If you are doing this, please do not consider yourself a professional because you are not. Now a good book that goes into standard measurements is *The Apparel Design and Production Handbook* (A Technical Reference). This book is available on our website – Shop.StartingaClothingline.com.

Your spec sheet per style in the sample size should include the following information:

- Your Company Name
- Style number
- Style name
- Size range that the style will come in
- Date at the time the spec sheet was finished (important)
- Measurements
- Special Instructions
- Fabric Choice
- Color Reference using Pantone Numbers
- Care Instructions and Placement
- Whether the style should come with hangtags
- Packing Instruction
- Any other relevant information

The Apparel Design Handbook will help you create your specifications and grading charts. **Grading** goes like this. Say you have a sample that will be created in size thirty-four. You want to carry those same qualities of fit to other sizes, such as thirty-six, thirty-eight, forty, and so on. Grading would come up with the measurements for the other sizes based on size thirty-four's (sample size in this case) measurements. It is scientific in nature and very important. We must recommend that you follow the Spec book until you fully understand the process. You could also hire a professional to do your grading. Most pattern makers and graders use Computer Aided Design **(CAD)** software to accomplish this task. It is somewhat expensive to have a professional do it, but may very well be necessary. You can ask your manufacturer to do the whole grading process, but this is not a widespread practice.

Manufacturers will need your grading chart per style to come up with your unit price per item. Please keep in mind that your total quantity ordered per style will influence your unit price on that style. In the beginning stages, you should not do more than four to six size variations of per style.

Creating a **master pattern** is the next phase. A master pattern is your standard blueprint of your custom fit. Master patterns can speed up your sampling as well as allow your manufacturers to have better accuracy at hitting your target measurements. Professional firms exist that can make master patterns for you. Again, this is a little expensive depending on your budget. You can get by without having a master pattern in the beginning. One reason for this is that you really do not know what your ultimate fit will be per style anyway. It will take a couple of production runs and sampling before you get to a firm set of measurements that you and your customers will really like.

Upon completing your designing stage, you should have the following:

- A plain sketch showing front, back and side views
- A technical sketch showing the details with measurements on it
- A specification sheet that can be done on programs like Microsoft Excel
- A grading chart that can also be done on programs like Microsoft Excel

This information will be transmitted to your manufacturer for sampling and production. If the manufacturer also requires a sample, have one made by you or a local seamstress. **A local seamstress** is good because it allows you to see your design come to life rather quickly versus waiting for a manufacturer do it.

The next phase of design is your labels, hangtags, and buttons, better known as trims. These are very important in terms of your branding. Look at other labels to get an idea of how and what should be on your labeling program. The joy of seeing something made with your button on it will feel very nice. Most people feel like they are really making it big when this happens. It is a temporary accomplishment, so enjoy it and then get back to the real work.

Labeling and buttons can be done here in the United States, but it is very expensive. We did some woven inner labels in the U.S. and it was not that expensive; however, we ended up not using these products because we did not like the design we had on them. MAKE SURE YOU REALLY LIKE YOUR LABELING PROGRAM BEFORE YOU SEND IT INTO PRODUCTION. Your overseas manufacturer may be the best choice for having your labels produced and the least expensive. An overseas manufacturer can produce labels as part of the order.

In coming up with the designs you want to bring out, you should get the feedback of people around you as well as strangers. Sometimes it is even necessary to act like it is somebody else's design just to get honest opinions. Some people may say they like something that they really do not. They may like it but would not necessarily buy it if they saw it in a store. Getting feedback is a great thing to do. Utilize it. Do not get mad if someone does not like what you have produced. **You cannot satisfy everybody's tastes!**

Do not worry too much about people stealing your designs. It happens. Just try to stay ten steps ahead. Manufacturers always state that they keep your designs private, but who really knows for sure? We have been bootlegged twice now and copied once. Why? We were the first to come up with a couple of great ideas. There is not really too much you can do about people knocking off your designs.

Designs cannot be copyrighted or patented unless you have something very unique, such as the mechanism we put on all our jogging suits. The best way to ward off copycats is to establish the fact that you were first to do something by getting it in national magazines and other wide-ranging media outlets. Draw as much attention to your garments as possible.

Most people in fashion, from the big companies to the small, are cookie cutters. They want to see what the next company is doing; they all follow the same trends. Many of them even share the same designers. Have you ever wondered why so many lines look alike? The big ones can get away with this because they have a lot of advertising behind them that pushes their brand into the public eye. Those designers just starting out cannot win through this strategy, so strategize differently. Another thing about designing is finding a middle ground in detailing. Detail is very important, but do not overwhelm your styles with too much detail, either. Complicated styles cost! It will also increase the chances of a manufacturer not wanting to make it, or worse, they may drop the ball in production. If you are planning on doing one-of-a-kind pieces, you will not need a manufacturer.

Structuring the Proper Team

When developing a clothing line, it is important to structure the proper team of people. The purpose of your team is to aid you in performing the daily tasks that you will be faced with when starting a clothing line. Through our experience, we have found it to be overwhelming for one or two people to accomplish the necessary tasks.

So you must bring together a team of individuals interested in developing a clothing line. This task is easier said then done, but it is not impossible. When choosing individuals for the team, it is very important that you use sound judgment. It is best to start your team with the right group of people; this will be beneficial in the long run.

Okay, what type of people should you look for? How many do you need on your team? It has been our experience that four to
five people can get the job done, but they must be solid.

What I mean by solid is all five people will have to perform. Below are the type of positions you should seek to fill and the characteristics needed for each one:

1. A person(s) with administrative skills.

This job consists of book keeping, budget forecasting, and

customer service, among other skills.

2. A sales person

This person(s) should be a very outgoing "people" person.

3. Distribution Manager

This person will handle the shipping and delivery of your

garments to local and out of town clothing stores.

4. Marketing / Public Relation (PR)

This will be the person who goes after magazines,
newspapers, television shows, movie productions, plays,
and radio stations. Her task will consist of product
placement deals for your garments, editorial write-ups
for your line, and interviews.

5. Spec Person / Designer

This person, which could be you, must be responsible for the

full scope of designing, quality assurance, and communication

between your company and your manufacturer(s).

I want to inform you of a job that belongs to everyone on the

team: promotions. All team members should be concerned with promotions. Every chance you get, you should be in the business of promoting. You should keep post cards on you at all times. We have a saying among our group: "A post card opportunity." This means that when you are around your target market, an opportunity exists for you to present them with a post card, and you should. Visit our business links page for resources.

Okay, now where do you find the individuals for your team?

You are the best person to answer this question. I can only offer suggestions at this point. One option you have is filling some of your positions with interns from your local colleges or design schools. By using interns, you can avoid payment due to the fact that they work to gain the necessary experience for graduating credits. One thing to keep in mind is this: do not expect or ask interns to design your line without paying them. This practice could come back to haunt you. Also note that schools will not give you interns unless you have an office—not your home—for them to work in.

Another suggestion for team members would be family members, friends, close associates or co-workers who you feel have something to offer to the team. Starting a clothing line can be very exciting and rewarding, but there is a lot of work involved, so be sure to assemble the proper team. You could also recruit from employment websites like monster.com, but finding professionals will cost you, so be sure you can handle the payroll if you take this route. Very few professionals you find will be willing to work for free. In fact, we are confident in saying that 99% of them will not.

Now you have taken a few steps to get your feet wet. You have created your brand and you have completed your business plan. You have samples and visuals. Thus far, you have probably paid for all of these things out of pocket or between yourself and partners. Pooling together your existing job incomes, tax returns, and money from friends and family should have been able to get you this far. You may also have raised money from selling T-shirts, hats and accessories.

Now you are ready to focus your thoughts on getting more financing to take you to the next phase. This is the hard reality that you may or may not be ready for. People around you who are uninformed will tell you that since you have a business plan, you will be able to get a loan. Not true. There are many other factors involved. You could actually have orders from stores and a bank account showing that you have been making money, yet still be unable to get a business loan.

So why can't you get that business loan? Fashion is an intangible business, meaning it is an idea. Banks do not loan money for ideas alone. The banks would rather loan you money to buy a building or equipment. The problem with that is, you need money to finance your production and other business expenses. Banks want collateral, plain and simple. Having a building that they can take back from you if you default on your loan works for them. If you have some equity in a home or financial bonds to put up against the loan, they will be more inclined to loan you money. You will also need some cash reserve as well.

You will then go through the approval process, which, they will tell you, will take a certain number of days. Then there is more paper work. You are looking at around two to three months to get anywhere. There will also be a lot of stipulations and hurdles for you to jump through. But it can be done.

The bottom line is you need collateral no matter what type of loan you want or end up getting. Some banks do have non-collateral based loans, but the amounts given are minute. So what if you want to take an easier route than getting a traditional business loan? A home equity loan is your best bet; you can have this type of loan in less than thirty days. Either way you go, you will have to put your house up.

If you do not have a house of your own, you will definitely have to figure something out. Putting a house up is a very big step. Therefore, before doing it, you should try financing your business with credit cards like Robert Townsend once did with his first movie. There is a reason we did not talk about financing earlier in this book. In the beginning, you really do not know how much money you will need. In general, no one can tell you how much money you need but you.

This business eats money very fast. Donald Trump once said that even the best laid plans don't go according to plan. Concrete planning must be fully strategized before borrowing large amounts of money from any person or institution. Try to make it as long as possible before taking this step.

Things to consider in coming up with an amount you need are: production runs, shipping, advertising, cash flow projections and tradeshow cost. Words of wisdom are to BORROW AND ACCEPT CREDIT WITH CAUTION! Too much credit and borrowing could come back to haunt you if your line does not do what you projected it to do or when you projected it to do it. The bottom line is you have to be willing to take risk to make it. You just want to make sure you are making well thought out decisions. Many designers seem to think that a bigger clothing brand would be interested in financing start up lines like yours. You would be surprised at how many people come to us with this approach. Most of them are now interested in financing or helping you with your line. There are few exceptions to this rule unless you know them personally. Do not ever ask this of any clothing company again!

If a bigger player becomes interested in your line, it will be because your clothes are selling very well, as in the case of Liz Claiborne buying Enyce. They have to see where they can immediately start to benefit from picking up your line. Large investors are the same way. Your catchy name and logo will not break this rule. They will also want to see that your line is not a fad and that you have at least a two-year track record of success. Either way, you should not count on getting your line picked up.

Smaller investors are good in the beginning stages, as long as you make sure they are not attached to your business for the long run. Someone should not be able to buy into your business for the long term with a couple of thousand bucks. You will be sorry later if you do make it and have a bunch of people in your business that got in for pennies.

Short-term loan contracts where you agree to pay them back in a certain amount of time are good. Make sure the people loaning you money are doing so with money that they have saved up so they do not pressure you to pay them back too quickly. Make sure beyond a doubt that you will be able to pay them back when you promised.

You will have to see the manufacturing, cash flow and advertising sections before finally coming up with the amount you may need to get your company fully off the ground. **You will have to play this game intelligently if you want to win. Just reading this guide alone proves you are one step ahead.**

OVERSEAS MANUFACTURING

We are now on the great subject of overseas manufacturing. Many designers think this is the key to their success. They believe once they have an overseas manufacturer, their business is officially launched and good times are ahead. They believe that now with some hot designs, they will have instant success. Do not get caught up in this premature thinking. Manufacturers will come and go. In Volume Two, we go into great depth about relationships with overseas manufacturers. Here in Volume One, we provide you with basic information only, but enough so that you can get things underway with manufacturers abroad.

Because people feel we are approachable, we have been asked many times to help people find manufacturers. The funny thing is, we know some of these people personally. Most of them have no clue about specifications, or anything else for that matter. This is stupid. They do not know anything about this business, but want a manufacturer! Donald Trump, whom we love to listen to, stated that his father told him when you are going into a business, you should try to know as much as you can about that business.

Before looking for a manufacturer, you should have your game plan together. Manufacturers can smell fresh blood and they will take advantage of you if you do not know any better. There are many areas to cover in terms of dealing with manufacturers. Would you go to a builder and tell him to build a building without having a blueprint? You have to know your stuff or have others on your team who do. We will tell you where to find overseas manufacturers in this section, but first let's cover some of the basics.

First, have your technical packs together per style, as we discussed in the design section. Next, have your labeling program together with sketches and size references. For instance, what is the size of buttons you will be using? The spec guide we mentioned earlier will help you in this area as well. **Get The Fashion Business Center for Spec Sheet Templates!**

Manufacturers will want to know some of the following:

- Your RN number ✓
- Information on your company ✓
- What type of items you make ✓
- Your website address ✓
- Your quality program
- Your mailing address
- Your shipping account number (Fed Ex or UPS, for example)
- How you will be paying for the order
- Your target price per style sent
- Your ship mark
- The delivery date you want per style
- How you want your goods packed
- The quantity of each style you want ordered (also per color)
- Your marketing plan in some cases
- Your financial status in some cases

- The amount of retailers you have in some cases

Manufacturers will evaluate working with you based on all of these things. Upon contacting them, have your standard introduction letter ready. We have a sample introduction letter in the back of the book for your review.

Now let's get into more specifics that we have not covered. Paying for your order is a big ordeal for you and the manufacturer. Manufacturers are worried about you paying and you are worried about paying someone across the globe and not getting what you want. In general, the manufacturer wants to be paid on what is called an **Irrevocable LC (Letter of Credit).** This is a document issued from you and your bank that guarantees the manufacturer that they will get paid for making your order.

So what is the catch with getting a LC? Remember, you may not have an official business loan. Getting a LC without this type of loan is almost impossible unless you have collateral (yes collateral, again). The bank will also look into your personal and business credit to approve you for getting a LC. The funny thing is, you could actually have enough money in the bank to cover the whole order, but cash is not considered collateral. (*New Edition - Update Alert: We have discovered a new and safer approach to paying manufacturers – almost like an LC. See Manufacturing Section in Chapter II*)

Make sure you make your manufacturer agree to meet your requirements as well keep their right to payment. Such things may include delivering in a certain time frame and upholding a certain level of quality. This practice should be done regardless of your payment method. The other route to payment when you do not have a LC is to do

payment by TT. Payment by TT is simply using your bank to wire funds to the manufacturer's bank account. They will give you all the necessary information you need (for example, their account number and routing information) to be able to do this. Your bank will charge you between $10 and $30 to wire money to a foreign account.

To get a manufacturer to agree to accept a wire for payment is a bit challenging. The reason is that with this type of transaction, there is no guarantee – in the eyes of the manufacturer – that you will pay the manufacturer for the order. Paying by wire can be done though. Just be sincere and prove to your business partners that you will pay in full. Normally you send the manufacturer a down payment to start the order and then pay around 80-100% of the total value of the order before it even leaves the manufacturer's country. These actions are usually enough to convince the manufacturer to accept a payment by wire. Do not forget, meanwhile, about the credibility of your new business partner. Make sure that you investigate the manufacturing company to the fullest before sending any money. Visit its website and cross reference its name through other directories. Ask the company what other brands it has worked with in the U.S. The key point is to investigate enough so that you are comfortable.

One thing that should concern you when choosing a manufacturer is how long it will take to process your order from start to finish. This is negotiable to a certain extent. The following is a breakdown of typical time frames:
Step 1:

Send your information on each style. You should send additional information such as artwork, hangtags and care label instructions as well. Always ask the manufacturer to offer its opinion on garment care options. You will have to choose the color and fabric for your main labeling program. In general, most companies use twill or satin woven labels.

Step 2:

First sample (fit sample). It will take a manufacturing company three to six weeks to make the first sample, despite what its managers may tell you.

Step 3:

Production will only begin after you approve the sample and have paid your deposit and/or presented your LC. If the sample is not a good representation of your specifications, then you will have to request another sample before going into production. It may take you one to two days to fully access the sample and have a fit session with a fit model. The manufacturer at this point will also send you swatches of fabric to choose from.

Step 4:

In general, manufacturers will tell you that they take anywhere from 40-90 days to manufacture an order after sample and fabric is approved. After manufacturing the order, the manufacturer will send you a production sample. This sample is very important because it represents what you will be getting. Ask the manufacturer to send production samples in every size that you ordered. After you approve a final production sample, it is time to have the order shipped back to you.

Step 5:

Next, you must decide how you want your order shipped. If you ship by air, it is faster and far more expensive than shipping by sea. Shipping by air will take anywhere from two to nine days. Shipping by ocean can take between 28-45 days. Shipping by air is about three to four times the price of shipping by ocean.

Step 6:

Getting your goods cleared through customs. We will discuss this a little more in the shipping section. In general, it can take anywhere from two to ten days to get your goods cleared through customs.

Step 7:

After customs clearance, your goods are trucked to your warehouse. You must inspect your merchandise for quality and quantity. The next step is to pack your orders and prepare to ship. Shipping to your accounts by ground services (recommended) will take an average of two to five days.

Basically, the above represents the time frame of moving from sample to getting your product inside stores. As you see, at the very fastest rates (which means shipping by air), it will take somewhere around 80 days to get your product out, and this is considered good. Things happen and never really go according to plan. In reality, expect the process to take 120 days. You may get lucky from time to time. With this information, you must carefully plan your releases to make sure they fall in the right season.

Manufacturers should follow your specs within a certain tolerance or be penalized. If they totally mess up on your order, make sure you have yourself covered in the contract. In return for a mistake on the manufacturer's part, you could demand a full refund plus shipping and any customs duties you paid.

To begin an official order with a manufacturer, you will issue an official purchase order for the manufacturer to sign. In the purchase order, both you and the manufacturer are agreeing to the price, delivery dates, and quantities per style. We have a sample purchase order at the back of the book for your review. You will issue a separate contract with your quality provisions for the manufacturer to sign. You should make sure that the manufacturer gives you weekly updates on your order. You will want to make sure you have all of the manufacturer's contact information, including his or her cell phone number.

Make sure the manufacturer sends you **lab dips** for the colors you have chosen. These are very important as they allow you to determine if the manufacturer is hitting your desired color on the mark. Make sure you let the manufacturer know to use quality dyes that **fully set into the garment** to avoid color bleeding and fading during cleaning.

QUALITY

Quality is one of biggest issues in terms of dealing with a manufacturer. Most manufacturers you meet will try to sell you on their quality practices. They will state that they are ISO 9000 and so on. It means nothing! Make sure your samples are good enough for you to want to do business with them and that they have excellent communication.

Quality is the standard of excellence and refinement. If you cannot visit the factory and oversee the manufacturing of your garments, maintaining quality will not be an easy process. The manufacturer will ship you initial garments called 1st samples. Each item is to be inspected for quality assurance. This is very important to the final development of your products. In order to perform this task, you must learn what to look for. Here is a list of items to commit to memory when checking samples:

- Measurements are correct (Also use fit model to test garment)
- Logos are in the right place
- All things that should be on the garment are there
- Check for coloring issues if the garment is actual fabric
- Check for loose, broken and crooked stitching
- Check buttons by pulling on them to make sure they do not come off
- Check zipper by sliding up and down a few times
- Make sure fabric is draping properly
- Check that garments are without funny smells
- Wash the garment or dry clean to test the cleaning method process

- Note any shrinkage or color change problems from the cleaning method
- Document your findings on your spec sheet and send this back to the manufacturer

Remember quality is very serious, and the lack of it can destroy your business overnight. Eat, drink, and sleep quality.

LANGUAGE BARRIERS

As you begin to contact manufacturers overseas by email, you will find that their written English is pretty good. Of course, there will be times when they may not fully understand you. Picking up the phone to call them is recommended from time to time. We find that talking on the phone is great for building communication and trust between you and your manufacturer.

Going overseas to personally meet with your manufacturer is a good investment as well. This trip will give you a chance to bond together, which could lead to greater quality in manufacturing. During your visit overseas, it is good to point out some of the things you like about the garments you are designing. You should also bring your manufacturer's attention to some of the things you do not want to see happen with your garments.

Point out mistakes that you do not want the manufacturer to make. Of course, traveling overseas for this is a little expensive, but well worth it in the long run. (Side Note: Many large companies send their people very often or have an employee stationed overseas to monitor quality.) Make sure you and the manufacturer have an order on the table before you go. Otherwise, it could end up a waste of time and money if you do not actually begin working with them when on their home turf.

If you cannot afford to go overseas but you have some critical information to give regarding the details of one of your designs, you could try the following. **Video record** an up-close look at the garment to help the manufacturer understand how you want it made. Send the manufacturer the Video. You will find this cheaper than traveling abroad. You can also cover a lot of areas on the Video to get them to understand your likes and dislikes when it comes to manufacturing your styles.

RECEIVING SAMPLES FROM OVERSEAS

Receiving samples most of the time is a great thing. When the samples do not look like what you want, it can be a let down, especially after paying around $75 to $150 in shipping costs. In general, overseas samples are not as cheap as you think. Manufacturers will charge you between two and three times the FOB unit price for the sample, plus any special processing they had to do to create the sample. Then add your shipping costs on top of that.

So if you agree that a pair of jeans will cost you $15 each, then you will end up paying $30 or $45 for the sample. Some will charge you up front and some will not. Some will deduct your payment for samples from your total order cost once you order those styles.

There are a few things to remember about getting your manufacturer to make your samples. Try not to overburden him or her with every style you have ever designed. Manufacturers are very busy and sampling costs them more money than they are charging you. Only send them items you have forecasted to go into production. Do not just send them a style because you just want to see how it looks. The other reason why you should not send so many styles at once is that they easily lose focus. You want to give them a few styles in the beginning to work on and see how they do with them.

After they make your sample, they will ask you for your shipping account number to send you the samples. Now for those of you who do not know about customs, here is a little lesson. Once again you will see that we give you the information that you will not find anywhere else. I know you are thinking this guide so far has been worth the price, right? Bringing in garments is like you traveling to another country and needing a visa.

The way to get around needing a visa for samples is simple. You can have your manufacturer cut a small but noticeable hole in the garment. The next step is for the manufacturer to write on the garment directly: "mutilated sample." Have you ever gone to a fashion show and wondered why some of the garments had holes in them? This is why.

The other thing you could do is have the word "sample not for sale" written on the garment in big letters. Yes, this means that you cannot model around town in these samples. Basically, the government just wants to make sure you will not be selling these samples without paying your duties on them. You may ask why not just pay the couple of dollars of duty to get some uncut samples? The visa is why. Visas cost money. Accept your abused garment and move on.

Now your manufacturer will have to send a commercial invoice with the samples that details the price you are paying for samples, country of origin of samples, and description of samples. It must also state that the samples are not for resale. We have a sample of this for your review at the end of the book. Also note, you will have to do the same thing if you are sending samples to the manufacturer.

ESTABLISHING PRICE PER UNIT

Agreeing on the FOB price (FOB simply means the price you pay without shipping included) is a big deal. FOB price depends mostly on how complicated your style is, the quantity that you want to order, the fabric, cutting and sewing, and packaging. Some manufacturers quote the price in CIF (CIF is getting the goods from their factory to a specified port near you). In general, always make them quote your price in FOB terms. FOB price should be given in two parts - one for the garment itself and one that includes the quota price.

Quota price could add another $1 to $5 per garment. **Always ask the manufacturer if the quota is included in the price** they quote you on each style. Some manufacturers will give you low prices to bait you and then later tell you that they did not add the quota to it. Some manufacturers will even quote you low prices then go up on them after making the samples. Expect this but do not let the price go too far up. On a good note, the quota system is supposed to begin phasing out in 2005. This will make your imported garments cheaper.

For your information, foreign manufacturers as a whole per country can only export so much of each category of clothing per year to the U.S. The exact numbers are controlled by both governments. Manufacturers have to purchase the quota from their government and then pass on the charge to you. Quota prices per category fluctuate all year long, going up and down. A good quota website can be found at: http://www.chinaquota.com/en/index.asp

FORECASTING PART I

How do you forecast what you want to order? We will look at this question in a simple way right now without any other outside factors. FOB unit price (including quota) plus shipping per unit plus U.S. duties give you your total price per unit.

For example, say a pair of jeans FOB price is $15. Shipping those jeans by air is $5 apiece. Say that the U.S. duty on those jeans is at a rate of 18% of FOB, which equates to $2.70. Your total price per jean, then, is $22.70. Next, suppose that the manufacturer wants you to buy 500 of this style. You are looking at a total investment of $11,350. Now you have to add your tops to that if you are doing tops. Then, say you are producing two jean styles and two top styles. Your investment for this order begins to add up very quickly. You are ultimately looking at spending around $30,000 to $40,000.

In general, overseas manufacturers can pull in all of the necessary inputs with which to make your products. They will source the fabric, materials, the washing and dying houses, packaging materials and so on. **Domestic production** sometimes forces you to pull all of the necessary resources together yourself. While there are few domestic producers left, domestic manufacturing has its advantages. Some benefits include shorter production time and shorter shipping times, and you can be more hands-on in achieving high quality levels. Sometimes the end price will not be that much different after you factor in all of the overseas expenses, such as quota, duties and shipping.

We will try to give you a few notes on pricing from overseas manufacturers. There are a lot of factors that determine the price you will pay per style. These factors include quantity, detailing, fabric, and wash detail, among others. Just to keep everything simple, let's look at a basic five-pocket pair of denim jeans with regular denim.

- If you order 500 to 1,000 units, your FOB price may be around $10 to $18 on average.
- If you order 5,000 per style, all the same color, your price may be around $8 to $14.
- If you order 50,000 pairs of jeans, you are looking at an FOB price of around $4 to $8.

U.S. duties prices vary per style / fabric / and country of origin. Check with your customs brokers for these rates. In general, most duties are between 10-24%. If you have a jogging set or some similar two-piece item, expect to pay a separate duty for the top and bottom.

SHIPPING

Now your product has been finished and it is time to ship. Keep in mind that by now you should have seen and approved the production samples and are 100% satisfied. The manufacturer will get with his or her normal customs broker or transportation specialist to arrange to have your goods shipped. Prior to finishing, the manufacturer should have asked you for the following information: your ship mark, how you want the goods packaged, the destination, and your method for shipping and paying the freight cost.

Some manufacturers will want you to pay shipping up front if they see any reason not to trust you. Most of the time, they will send freight to you COD. You have to tell your manufacturer how you want your goods packaged. In general, most companies put each piece in its own polybag, which is a clear plastic, sealed bag. Polybags should be of good quality and should not split easily. Written on the polybag should be your company name, the style number, RN number, color, country of origin and a message that states "this bag is not a toy and should be kept away from children."

Next, tell the manufacturer how you want your styles packed in the carton or box. Tell him to use very durable, high quality boxes. Advice: You will be able to reuse these boxes to ship your orders to retailers. Usually, companies pack by like color and size per style. Now you have to provide the manufacturer with your **ship mark** to put on the outside of the box. Ship mark information is your company name, address, country, RN number, style, color, size, and ratio per box.

Your goods are now set to fly out, if you have chosen air freight. Make sure you have **insurance** on the goods no matter how you ship them! Along with the cargo, the manufacturer should be sending the master visa, bill of lading, and commercial invoice, among other documents. The master visa is required to get the cargo into the U.S. The information on the visa must be fully correct. One important aspect of the visa is the category number.

Category numbers are issued from the government, which classifies each style of garment by style and fabric. Primarily, your manufacturer and customs broker will be responsible for this area. For example, men's T-shirts that are cotton are classified under category 347/348. Each category has a U.S. duty rate assigned to it as mentioned earlier.

Now it is your job to have a customs broker handle the shipment as it arrives into the U.S. **Customs Brokers** are responsible for dealing with U.S. customs to get your goods cleared. In general, it takes two to seven days to get your goods cleared through customs on a good run. Your customs broker will bill you for her services, plus the duty fees and the COD freight amount. A customs broker will not give you credit, so prepare to pay up front.

To find a custom house broker simply look in your yellow pages under customs brokers. Talk to them and see what their requirements are to set up an account. They will make you sign a power of attorney to give them the right to work for you. Just for your reference, the government requires you to have an **entry bond** on file to bring goods into the country. Make sure to ask your customs broker which plan is best for you in terms of bond choice. You can either choose between a single-entry bond or an annual bond. The single entry bond is the cheapest in the short run, but will end up costing you more depending on how many times you will be bringing orders in within that year.

We have purposely saved for last our information on how to find manufacturers. We feel that you should know about dealing with manufacturers before actually looking for one. We have made it possible for you to find and locate manufacturers all over by compiling our Ultimate Fashion Contact List.

This E-book has all of the manufacturing contacts you will need. Manufacturers are listed that make a full variety of apparel and accessories. Visit our web site for more information on this cool E-book.

Now that you know how and where to find manufacturers, it is necessary that you approach them in a professional manner. We stress again: know your stuff. At this point, you will begin submitting emails to various manufacturers.

Relay the following information:

- The name and location of your brand

- Who you are

- Your website address

- What garments you specialize in

- The type of quantities per style you are looking to have made

- Additional information on your brand

- The primary fabrics that you use

Note: We have a sample of this introduction in the back of this book, as mentioned earlier.

After manufacturers reply to you, ask them the following questions:

- What is their full contact information?

- What is their company's website?

- What garments and fabrics do they specialize in?

- What is their turnaround time?

- What is the amount of time it takes them to finish a sample?

- Do they comply with all child labor laws?

- What is their quality policy?

- Who will be your contact in terms of sending specs?

Then you will let them know your forecast for the styles you are about to send. Ultimately, you will discuss issues like delivery dates and payment processes. Keep the following in mind for future reference: **China has a month long holiday in February**. During this month, no work is done for the most part. This holiday will affect your samples, production, and delivery dates if you are having something made around that time. (Side note: Once again we are letting you know about things in advance so you can plan around them. We got caught off guard one time with this holiday.) You will email and send your garment information to them. Sometimes they will want you to send them samples of the actual garments and fabric swatches. In this case, you or the local seamstress will have to make them.

YOUR BRAND'S IMAGE

Creating your brand's image is very important. Without a good image, your clothes may not sell. What exactly is image? Image starts with your name, the look of your website, the look of your hangtags, the look of your clothes, and the look of your business cards. You want others to view your line as you do. Creating professional representations to back you up is essential.

One area of concern is making sure you have **the right models**. Finding models is hard, contrary to popular belief. We have seen the best looking people look horrible in print. Remember this, some people have great smiles but do not look as good when they have to make a straight face picture.

In general, we have mostly used models that were not from modeling agencies. We like to use everyday people; there are definitely advantages and disadvantages to this approach. Modeling for print is like acting on film: some people are poor actors and it shows. Basically, we recommend that if you are going to use amateurs, you should pay them little to nothing for their first shoot. Their first shoot will allow you to evaluate them for future hire.

If the model does well the first time, he or she should definitely be paid the second time around. Most amateur models will model for free just to get free photos for their portfolio and exposure. You must make them sign a release before shooting that releases the pictures to your company. In general, it has been our practice that we have total rights to the pictures and can use them in any of our advertising campaigns with no restrictions. We give models the right to obtain the pictures for their portfolio. Look for models at work, clubs, concerts, modeling agencies and elsewhere. Just make sure they represent your target market and are reliable.

The photographer is another important factor in creating your image. A good photographer must be able to capture your models and garments with great clarity. Nothing is worse than a blurry picture you tried to turn into an ad. You can find photographers in the yellow pages, by talking to stores in your area, asking models, or inquiring at your local colleges. Make sure when finding a photographer you see their portfolio. They must sign a release, too, before the photo shoot but usually you have to agree to their terms. If they have too many restrictions on the use of the pictures, you may either deal with it or find someone else with fewer restrictions, or none at all. Many just want you to give them photo credit (their name written in the margin of a print ad – usually written as "photos by …"), in addition to paying them for the photo shoot and film processing. In general, the better the photographer, the more restrictions on use and the higher the fees.

The Make-Up Artist is also a key person in creating the right image on print. A make-up job can make or break a photo shoot. Find make-up professionals the same way you would find a photographer. You can also find make-up artists in a large department store's make up department. Be sure to look at their portfolio. During the photo shoot, make sure the make-up job is tailored to the model and the outfit he or she will be wearing.

In general, photo shoots can be done anywhere. You can do them in the studio or on location. If you are just taking a few pictures here and there without a lot of people and lighting equipment, you can get by without a city permit. If you are planning on the lights, cameras, action and require that streets are blocked, then contact your local city government to get a permit.

Now that you have finished your photo shoot, it is time to pick the pictures that you want to use in your campaign. Pick wisely, taking notes of the good and bad details of each picture. Just in case you did not know this, we will tell you – ALL PICTURES USED IN ADS HAVE BEEN TOUCHED UP. A good touch up job is essential to the pictures you choose to go with. Find a graphic artist to do this. Do not put out un-touched-up pictures. You will use touch up services to eliminate and improve certain details in the picture(s).

The next thing to do is put together your ads, website and press kits. Use your touched-up pictures to create each one of these. You may use a graphic artist to create these if you are unable to yourself. In general, doing things yourself is good because it saves you money. However, there is a learning curve, and while you may think that you are good at something, only time will tell. Think about how many times you may have looked at something you did a year or two ago, and now you look at it like, "What I was thinking?" It takes awhile to really get good at something.

Advertising

Advertising and marketing are important pieces of the puzzle. Without the right mix of advertising and marketing initiatives in place, your brand may find it hard to fly. First, it is important to know your target market. Who is your customer? What are your demographics? After you identify your target, you must plan how to reach it so that it knows you exist. In reality, you have two types of customers: your retailers and your end customer who buys from retailers.

You must run successful campaigns that target each of your customers. Print ads in national magazines are expensive. The best approach to them is to pay up front. Do not accept credit from them if you really cannot afford it. If you are planning on your future sales revenue to give you the cash to pay for the ad after they run it, you should think again. Remember, that even the best laid plans do not always go accordingly. You could end up in the hole.

Magazines will offer you a better rate if you agree to run in a certain amount of their issues. In your beginning two years, you should be very careful on all of the financial commitments you make. Our advice is to first ask them to run the first ad for free or at a nicely reduced price to allow you to see if you are really reaching your market through their magazine. Upon the success of the first run, you then structure an agreement to run more ads.

Our advice again is to never do back-to-back ads during your first two years in the same magazine. Always space your ads by at least one month apart to see the effectiveness of each ad. Never agree to more than two to three ads per contract. Our advice will save you in the long run unless you have money flowing out of your socks.

The other thing to know about getting a good rate is that in general nobody pays the magazine's published rate. Some will insist that you pay the published rate, but even so, try to get around it if you can. You will have to sell them on the fact that you will be doing repeat business with them for the long term if you get a good response and sales level from being in their publication. You could also look up a discount advertising broker. This will also help get you better rates on your print ads.

Your advertising and marketing campaign could also include doing radio and Internet ads, sponsorships, fashion shows and other promotional activities. Just make sure all of your advertising makes sense. Make sure you are letting the customers connect and identify with your products and image. You should make sure all of your ads have your contact information and website. Postcards should also be used to get your message out. They are inexpensive and if done right can lead to sales. Postcards should indicate where a person can go to see your product.

Larger firms advertise many times just to keep their brand name in the consumer's face. Starting out, you will want to advertise because you need to sell your product. Selling is the lifeline of your company. Image is something that should be added to your ad, but the main focus should be your product. Timing is everything as well. For instance, say in your ad there is a model wearing a hot dress. Your best bet is to have that ad appear at the same time that the dress is in stock.

People who like the dress will call you to order it. This is a good thing. What happens if you were just doing the dress in the ad to get attention and establish brand recognition? Then you would have people calling for the dress only to hear you say, "we do not have that dress." At this point, you would probably try to get the dress produced. But it will take you around three months or more to get it in. By that time, your major demand has drizzled away and the season has changed. You lost! To get a catalog that lists most magazines and their rates, visit: mediamanager.com, or call 203-259-8100.

Another key area to mention in terms of generating buzz for your brand is using promotions. You can have various contests to bring customers into your show room and retail locations.

The days of using celebrities to market your line are very limited. Why? Most celebrities now have their own lines. If they do not, they may want to charge you a nice endorsement fee. If you can find a celebrity who will wear your clothing from time to time, it is a good thing and it should not cost you anything. You can use the event of a celebrity wearing your clothes as a part of your press release.

There are people who will tell you who they are or who they know, trying to leach on to your line and clothes. Be on the lookout for fakes; they are everywhere. We once had a fake stylist, who was supposedly working with Ludacris, and a well-known singer con us out of a few outfits. He presented information that made him look legitimate, but he turned out to be a bogus liar. Watch yourself.

Many new designers think of the LL Cool J story with Fubu and want to use music videos to blow their line up. Get that out of your head if you think like this too. If it happens like that – cool. But do not go around expecting it. Also, get this. Video directors and programmers now will not show your logo on your clothes unless you are a big brand name like Sean John or something. They have closed this avenue for the most part.

We once had our clothes in Eminem's "Lose Yourself" video and they edited so much that you could not even see our name. There was another time when a director stated that he could not put our clothes in the video because our logo was too big. Keep in mind that it was a small left chest type of logo. The best source of free exposure now is to try to get various television show hosts or actors to wear your product during taping. Contacting the wardrobe department could bring you this opportunity.

Basically, we are telling you that getting your brand off the ground will be hard work. Do not go expecting any easy workings. Many celebrity lines are even dying and falling off. Despite the celebrity association, they too are not exempt from the various challenges of starting a clothing line. You have to be smart. Reading this guide is your first step towards success. You can learn from our triumphs and mistakes. Knowledge is power.

Generating press is another key way to get your message to consumers. It is always better to have other people say good things about you than you yourself. You should approach fashion editors and stylists to inform them of new products you are bringing out. You should send out various press releases each season. Make sure you convey why they should cover your brand. Are you doing something exciting that will catch their attention?

Another key point of your advertising is actually called POP (point of purchase) advertising. Make sure your retail accounts have posters and postcards for their customers to see. Retailers will want this. Make sure your garments have distinctive hangtags on them. Convey your company's image to your consumers the best way possible.

Selling your products is the lifeline of your company. Without the proper sales, you will eat through your invested funds. If you do not sell out in a given time frame, it will weigh on your whole system. So it is imperative that you have your sales plan together prior to placing a production order with any factory.

Do not have thoughts like, "If I order 500 of a certain style, it will cost me $30, but if I order 1,000, it will only cost me $19." Okay, that could be fine. But do you actually have orders for that extra 500 or even the full first 500? Keep in mind that you will still be paying all the shipping and duties associated with the deal. The **fashion industry is a race against season**. It is your job to get a product in and sell out of it within its season. Over-ordering could leave you stuck with something past season and then you will have to discount it or not sell it all.

Now the key point here is that you have to have a good sales plan. Define your sales plan. To whom do you want to sell: retailers or consumers? If you just want to sell directly to consumers, you could open your own physical store. You could also sell from your website.

You may choose to sell to retailers and direct consumers. In Chapter Three "How to Sell Effectively to Retailers", we offer you help in this area. In general, selling to stores is tricky. Why? There are many factors involved in doing so. We will explain why in the next chapter.

Selling Your Products to Retailers Directly

In this section, we will discuss the basics you need to know in order to be successful. You should start off selling your clothing to stores in your area. Okay, let's begin!

First, I want to share with you some of my experiences I had when selling our clothing line to local stores. This will aid in giving you a general idea of what it is like selling and presenting your line to store owners and buyers.

I will make this quick and to the point. The very first time our line was presented to a clothing store, I was the sales representative. I walked away from my first appointment with no sales and some pretty discouraging words from the store owner. Needless to say, I did not allow this experience to hinder our progress. I continued to move forward, making other appointments. You should do the same. Adjust your sales approach if needed before going on your next appointment.

My second appointment turned out to be the exact opposite of the first one. This store owner wrote a big order. He had some very encouraging words and he invited us to be in his fashion show. Weeks later, the store from our first appointment called us back and wrote an order. The rest is history.

Now let's look at some of the fine points you will need to know when selling your clothing line in your local area. You should have a pen and paper handy when actually performing this task.

- Grab the telephone directory and turn to the clothing section.

- Begin calling the stores you see to find out what brands they carry. This will help you determine whether you want your line in this store or not. (Note: Do not identify yourself as a clothing line just yet.) You should want to sell your clothes around other brands similar to yours.

- Make a list of the clothing stores you found to be suitable.

- Call the stores from the list you have made and ask to speak with the owner or the buyer. When talking to the owner or manager, you should be very professional and excited about introducing your line to him or her.

- Start by greeting the owner, and then introduce yourself and the name of your clothing line.

- Let the owner know that you would like to set up an appointment to showcase the line.

- Present the line during the appointment and write up the order!

Note: Selling in-store is the very best method of sales for a new clothing line. It allows you the one-on-one interaction necessary to build a relationship and get the sale. Be sure to read Chapter Three for additional information and techniques.

TERMS TO RELAY TO RETAILERS

In general, you should look to sell your products to retailers on a COD basis. Some retailers do not like doing COD. They will ask you to give them credit. The bigger chains will definitely want credit. You should not extend credit to anyone if you do not have a factor that has approved them for credit. So what is a factor? **A factor** is a bank that buys your invoices from you at a fee. Basically, setting up a factoring deal works like this:

- You can find a factor by going though your local yellow pages, looking under banks and factoring.
- You can also try to find factors by using keywords like:
  - Google.com Keyword: Apparel industry factors, factoring, clothing industry factors, how to get a factor, factoring banks
- They will require you to tell them about your business type, monthly sales volumes, and so on. Find one that will work with you based on your projected sales and financial forecast.
- Next, find out their terms.
- Find out what they do when stores do not pay.
- Next, give them the names of stores you want to extend credit to.
- They will do credit checks on those stores.
- If the store is approved, the factor will buy their invoice from you.

How the process works is typically like this:

- You ship goods to the store that was approved by factor.
- The factor pays you around 80% of the total amount of that invoice within a day or two of the retailer receiving the order.
- The store then has to pay the bank instead of you, usually within 30 days.

After the store pays the bank, the factor will give you the balance of 20% minus their fee, which is typically around 3-5%.

This being said, I want to bring your attention to your overall net profit per unit. When you figure taking out another 3-5% per unit for factoring, how does your net profit look? If you cannot get a proper profit margin period, financial trouble could be ahead. You do not have to do credit, but not doing it limits your potential retail customer base. **Whatever you do, do not extend credit to a retailer on your own without a factor.**

The Paper Work Needed to Get Sales

You should create line sheets for each of your products. A line sheet is a paper that contains a picture of your product along with the selling features, such as sizes, price, colors, fabric, and delivery date. You will present this to the retail buyer for review and ordering. We have samples of line sheets in the sales guide that we offer.

FINDING ONLINE RETAILERS TO SELL YOUR PRODUCTS TO

Selling online is big business. You should be selling your products from your website as well as from other people's websites. To find online retailers, simply type in some other brand names into search engines. Contact the online stores you find. You could also do drop shipping deals with them if they do not necessarily want to invest in your product.

It seems that there is a big myth about how, if you do the Magic Tradeshow in Las Vegas, you will be set. The announcement that FUBU once processed $300,000 in orders out of a hotel room at Magic is what put this urban legend into effect. There are many things to take into account with respect to this tradeshow. We will begin to inform you and take you deep inside Magic.

The contact number to register to exhibit at Magic is:

818-593-5000. Magic has **two Tradeshows a year,** in **February** and **August**, and it is a **four-day event.**

Your time table for preparing for the Magic Tradeshow should run somewhat like this:

Step 1:

Ship your samples and other items to Magic in advance if you can not pack them all. You may need to buy oversized garment travel cases to pack all of your samples and materials. To get a catalog of some of the things you may need while exhibiting, visit travelautobag.com, or http://startingaclothingline.com/html/**fashionbusinesslinks**.html. Expect to pay extra at the airport for oversized baggage. You can get around this fee by spreading the weight out among your bags. Reserve your rental car in advance as well. Your place of pick up is the Las Vegas Airport. Be sure your rentals have all the cargo space you will need.

Step 2:

Reserve your hotel rooms far in advance. You should schedule to arrive at Magic one to two days prior to the show start date. If you arrive on the day before the show begins, make sure your plane gets in early that morning. The day before Magic is when most companies begin setting up their booths. You should plan on flying out of Magic either that last evening of the tradeshow or the next day.

Step 3:

After exhibiting on the last day, you will begin to pack up your materials at your booth. Visit a shipping company in Las Vegas, like Fed Ex, to ship your samples back home (at least the things you can carry on the plane with you).

So ultimately, anticipate spending at least five days in Las Vegas. There will be plenty of parties to go to. Have fun! But remember that you are there to work. Magic hours usually start around eight in the morning. Waking up that early is a hard thing to do after you have partied until 6 A.M.

Magic is expensive. Your basic booth space for each 10 x 10 area in your booth is around $3600. Your booth display, then, can cost you anywhere from $1300 to who knows what astronomical price. A nice looking booth display in a 10 x 10 area will cost you around $4,000, which still is far less than some of the others you will see there. Companies like Tommy Hilfiger have an area of about 80 x 80. Larger companies will have elaborate booth displays that reflect their brand's image. Most large companies probably spend at least around $35,000 or more on their booth. Once again, if your pockets are not loaded, do not get caught up in the hype. We have seen large and fancy booths that were empty. Good booths do not guarantee good sales.

A very good friend of ours who used to rep for Tripple Five Soul had the following advice: Magic is really for servicing your existing accounts. If you do not have people coming to see you at the tradeshow, then really you should not be there. Of course, we are all hard-headed sometimes. You will find very few of the major buyers stopping at booths they have not heard of. Even having a national ad out at the time of Magic does not mean retailers will stop in to see what you have to offer.

Many people pay Magic to put up displays in the hallways and hang banners at different places around the convention site. Some put banners on taxi cabs or buses. Our advice is to save your money. Use that money in more needed areas – and there are plenty of those. So your investment in Magic entails shipping your samples in, transportation, hotel, and meal costs, paying for team members to participate, setting up your booth, reserving your space, and preparing your models. These expenses will quickly add up to $10,000 at a minimum.

You will hear this only from us, right here in this guidebook. One of the best benefits of going to Magic, besides the chance of securing orders, is their registry. You will have all types of manufacturers contacting you after exhibiting at Magic. Magic also offers a separate show where designers can go to meet with manufacturers. This show goes on at the same time as Magic. (Ask Magic's management about their manufacturers show.) You could also visit the Asap show, which also takes place during Magic, to find manufacturers. Visit Asap ahead of time at asapshow.com. **Remember, manufacturers**

who contact you are more likely to work with you in the end than those who do not take the initiative and were instead contacted by you.

Now how do people draw booth traffic at Magic? They pass out postcards, for one thing. They have models walking around wearing their clothes. They mail out information to retailers to advertise their booth prior to the show. They also try to grab people's attention as they are walking by at the tradeshow. Finally, they use promotions and celebrities at the booth to raise interest. Many of the celebrity based tactics, however, draw more spectators than buyers.

In general, none of these tactics really work. We have seen Mike Tyson and Redman at Magic booths. Sure, the crowds drew to see these celebrities, but the attention did not result in booth attendants actually writing orders. The bottom line is, you have to have a hot line before you even get to Magic to be successful at Magic. For the record, do not expect major department stores to stop at your booth just because you are at Magic. In general, they visit their big brand names and then head for the door. All of this being said, there will be times when buyers are looking for new lines and may stop in to hear your sales pitch. Present your line well and you could be writing up a nice size order. Local and Regional Tradeshows are cool to do as well. They are less expensive than Magic. To find out more about them, ask your local retailers about the various shows they attend. Local tradeshows are without the glitz of Las Vegas's Magic. Nevertheless, it does not matter what show you do – you must have a hot line to have major success at any of them.

DETERMINING YOUR PRICE STRUCTURE (Wholesale and Retail)

Price is everything. When you set your prices for your collection, there are many things to take into account. Your price must be a reflection of your bottom line. Your price to retailers should be around one and a half to two times your total unit price. The retail price consumers will pay should be keystone plus $2. Keystone simply means doubling the price. So if you sell a pair of jeans to a retailer for $30, the consumer should be paying around $62 for that pair of jeans.

Things get tricky based on the current market price for a pair of jeans in your target market segment. Say your main competitor is somebody like PEPE jeans, and PEPE jeans is selling their jeans to retailers for $32. Because they are an established brand, they are making the store money. The store, therefore, will not want to pay more for your unproven product. You will have to convince them why they should invest more money into your jeans.

So, suppose you decide you need to sell your jeans at a wholesale price of $32 to get retailers to buy. If you recall, your jeans are costing you $22.70. Your net profit is $9.30, which is far from doubling your money. Now assume you have a sales rep you are paying who is earning 10% commission against the unit price. Your sales rep would be making $3.20, leaving you with a net profit of $6.10 per jean. Remember as well the factoring charges, if you are doing any factoring. This does not sound good, does it?

How can you better your profit margin? Start shipping by sea instead of air, for one. In fact, more companies ship by ocean. This is easy to do as long as you do not mind waiting the extra time to get your order in. This could add $4 in additional net profit. The other way to better your profit margin is to order larger quantities. However, unless you are selling out, this is the wrong move to make. Do not get caught up in over-ordering. Not all the clothes you see at stores like TJ Maxx and other discount venues are there because they had defects. Some are plain victims of over-ordering – someone thinking a demand was going to be there when, in fact, it was not. Big name brands and celebrity lines are not exempt from this mistake.

Having a sales representative is a good thing in terms of getting orders outside of your local area. Finding industry sales reps, though, is a hard thing to do. Most sales reps will not take on your project because you are too new. If you have any of the following, such as major funding, contacts, celebrity endorsements, or a great advertising campaign under way, you may be able to score an industry vet. The good thing about an industry vet is that they have a network of retail contacts that can launch your product quite quickly in some cases.

You can still find and approach some seasoned industry vets by doing a little research. Look through local tradeshow books or visit trade shows. Be watchful for the ones who will take you to the bank whether they get you orders or not. In our sales book, we teach you how to find and train non-established industry reps to sell in the apparel industry. This in many ways will be your best bet for creating your sales force.

Now back to price. If you are a hot line in demand then you can get away with selling your jeans for $45 and make double your money. Your retail customer ends up paying $92. If you are not in demand, going at it like this will be a struggle. Ultimately you may end up dropping prices anyway. Sometimes even having much detail and luxurious fabrications will not get you out of the water with higher than average prices. With the right amount of advertising and press, it is possible to achieve the prices you want, though, so don't give up.

At the end of the day, you must use your actual orders and interested stores to forecast what you can comfortably move before ordering your clothes. It is better in the beginning stages **to not have enough** and sell out than to have too much. Ultimately you will want to make your line hot so that retailers and consumers come looking for you instead of the other way around.

Just as important as quality, on-time shipping, and sales are to a clothing line, so is the bottom line reflected through your cash flow. I cannot emphasis enough how many businesses in general do not have a good understanding of cash flow. It is the number one killer in a business if you do not understand it and cannot handle it properly. I will do my best to help you in this area. A good accountant can also help you.

Looking at cash flow is best done by creating a spread sheet forecasting all of your sales, cost of goods, and expenses. You must analyze your cash flow to be able to manage your growth. The best way to set this up is by doing an income statement that shows your net profit or loss per month. Below that, you insert your cash flow line showing your carryover balance at the end of each month. If it turns negative during any month, you will want to make some adjustments. We have an example of this in the second volume of this guide.

Your income statement should include figuring your cost per unit as well. Your styles should be forecasted on the statement as well. These include things such as FOB price, shipping, duty, number of units you are ordering, commission, wholesale price, gross amount you can make, and net profit per unit / per order.

Basically, you will have to have a good sense of your cash flow to be able to come up with the total amount you need to start your clothing line. If you know you only have a certain amount of money to produce your line, you should plan your cash flow accordingly. Projecting cash flow is also a part of your business plan. It is the main thing banks will want to see if you are taking the route of trying to get a business loan next to collateral.

In general, most businesses do not see significant net profits for the first five years of business. The reasoning behind this is that it takes time to get to know your market and learn how to run your business efficiently. (Side Note: Did you know that Phat Farm Clothing Company, which did $615 million in 2003, in the beginning had gone bankrupt before coming back to be successful?)

For additional information on cash flow and actual examples of income statements for the clothing industry, see Chapter Two, "The Real Reality of Owning and Operating Your Own Clothing Line."

WAREHOUSING and SHIPPING ORDERS

Now your product comes in and you must prepare to start shipping to stores. When the goods come in to your warehouse, you should inspect and count them to make sure everything is correct. Your warehouse should be clean and neat. Your warehouse location should be secure and kept secret.

Warehousing your merchandise can be quite simple and inexpensive depending on the route you take. I am going to explain to you the least expensive way to warehouse your product. Are you ready for this? The basement or garage, depending on the condition of either, is an economical place depending on your volume. Storing your merchandise in your own home is also a good move until you see exactly how your sales and revenues are going.

As your company grows, you should begin searching for warehousing space. Grab the telephone directory and look for storage companies in your area. Contact them and set up an appointment to see a few units to decide which size would be suitable for your shipments. There is a small cost involved, but a storage company will be less expensive than an actual warehouse. When the situation develops where your shipments outgrow your existing storage unit, it is best to upgrade to a bigger unit. When your shipments outgrow the bigger unit, then it is time to consider graduating to an actual warehouse.

No matter where you decide to store your garments, it is important to keep a watchful eye on them to avoid weather damage and other unfortunate incidents. It is also a good thing to make sure you have insurance no matter where you are housing your products.

Ship your orders to retailers and consumers using your specified carrier. Make sure to pack all orders correctly and neatly. Make sure to include all paperwork inside of each package, such as invoices and thank you letters. When sending your package to retailers, be sure to include your displays and promotional materials.

If you have a big department store chain as a customer, be sure to pay close attention to their shipping policies. Most have certain formats for you to adhere to. Non-compliance could close your account. They also require you to have UPC Barcoding tags as well. Find out their terms before seeking barcoding. For more information on how to get UPC Barcodes, visit:

http://startingaclothingline.com/html/**fashionbusinesslinks**.html
Also see Google Keyword: apparel label barcoding.

If you are not shipping to accounts that require this, you can hold off on getting them. For additional information on shipping to and dealing with retailers, see our two other guides.

Filing Your Taxes

Be sure to keep good bookkeeping records of all sales transactions and expenses. Pay
any taxes accordingly. File your taxes on time. The use of a good tax attorney is
essential. If you have been working a separate job in addition to your clothing line, you
could see some larger tax returns than normal if you have a net loss at the end of the
year.

Congratulations, you have made it through Chapter One! We are sure you know now how to start a clothing company. It is hard work, but the rewards can be great if you do it right. All of this information may be a little overwhelming at first, but read this guide a few times over to really let this knowledge sink in. We have covered the main areas essential in getting you going. Are you ready to command your share of this $90 billion dollar industry? Are you ready to get your designs out of your head and out to the world for others to see and love?

If you are truly serious about starting, as purchasing this guide suggests, then you must read our two other guides and gain the extra edge and strategy for success. If these guides had been available when we started, we could have saved a lot of money and time, and made better decisions all around. It is all up to you now. Are you the next hot fashion line in the making?

Sample Commercial Invoice

(Use something like this when you are sending samples to your overseas manufacturer – this is just an example. Yours may vary.)

Your Company Name

Your Company Address

Your Company Phone Number

Contact Person at Your Company

COMMERCIAL INVOICE FOR GARMENT SAMPLES / SWATCHES

Consignee

Manufacturer's Contact Info Here

Commercial Invoice Number 0000

Date: 0/00/00

Description 1: 1 swatch sheet with denim fabric: Total USD $0.00

Description 2: 100% cotton Men's denim pants – "Marked Mutilated Sample – Not for Resale". One pcs. Total USD: $1

Description 3: etc.

All samples contained in this shipment are U.S. origin.

(Note: Your manufacturer would put their country when sending you samples.)

Total Amount United States Dollar $1.00

Shipment by Fed Ex on 0/00/00

Airway Bill No: 0000-0000-0000

The shipment contains no solid wood packaging material

All goods and samples are of USA Origin

All samples have been mutilated and marked accordingly.

Paper and Sample are of No Commercial Value

Invoice For Customs Clearance Purposes Only.

(Note: You would present to you your manufacturer when placing a order. This is just and example. Your information will vary)

PURCHASE ORDER #0000

DATE: 0/00/05
CONTRACTOR:
Contact Info:

CONSIGNEE:
Your information here.

TERMS:

DATE ORDERED: 0/00/2005
OFFICIAL DATE GOODS ARE TO BE READY TO SHIP: 00/00/2005

PAYMENT TERMS: TBD
LATE PENALTY SHOULD GOODS NOT SHIP BY OR ON DELIVERY DATE: TBD

NOTE: THIS CONTRACT IS NOT VALID WITHOUT VENDOR CONTRACT BEING SIGNED BY ALL PARTIES

STYLE ORDERED	# OF COLORS	FOB PRICE	UNITS	AMOUNT
MENS JEANS (STYLE 200)	1	$15.00	500	$7,500.00
MENS TOPS (STYLE 100)	1	$10.00	500	$5,000.00
TOTAL:				$12,500.00

QUANTITIES

STYLE ORDERED	COLOR:	S	M	L	XL	TOTAL PER COLOR
MENS TOPS STYLE 100	WHITE	1125	125	125	125	1500

STYLE ORDERED	COLOR:	30	32	34	36	TOTAL PER COLOR
MENS PANTS STYLE 200	BLUE	125	125	125	125	500

PO AGREED TO BY ALL PARTIES BELOW:

_____
AGENT NAME: PRINT

_____
SIGNATURE OF AGENT:

_____
SIGNATURE OF VENDOR CONTACT:

_____
PRINTED NAME OF VENDOR CONTACT:

_____
FACTORY NAME:

_____
YOUR SIGNATURE:

(SAMPLE INTRODUCTION LETTER TO SEND TO MANUFACTURERS)

(YOUR COMPANY NAME HERE)

WHAT WE LOOK FOR IN A MANUFACTURER

Greetings Sir or Madam,

How are you today? It is a pleasure to introduce ourselves to you today. We are (YOUR COMPANY). We design a full variety of designer styles for women including dresses, tops, jeans, T-shirts, and Sweaters (Whatever clothing or fashion styles that you make). We are a (Type of Brand – like denim, upscale, dress, menswear etc.) fashion company.

We are looking for a manufacturer that can meet our objectives in quality, delivery time and quantity. We are a (YOUR COUNTRY) brand currently advertising in (where are you advertising). We are in the midst of becoming a very well known brand here and need good manufacturing behind us. We are interested in long-term cooperation with a company that can fully meet our needs and is willing to work with us to build our brand further.

Please answer the following questions for us:

1. How long does it take to develop a sample?

2. What is the cost of developing a sample that we are charged?

3. What is your turnaround time once production order is placed? (We prefer 40 - 60 days production time or whatever time you prefer should be conveyed here.)

4. What is your quality assurance process?

5. Do you do men's and women's?

6. What is the minimum quantity that you will produce per style, per color etc.?

7. What fabrics to you specialize in (please list all)? (Denim, Knit, and Satin?)

8. What type of clothing do you specialize in? (Dresses, T-shirts, jeans?)

9. Where are your factories located?

12. Are you an agent or a manufacturer direct?

13. If you are an agent – what is your commission?

14. How fast can you quote pricing after receiving specs and sketches only (no samples) sent via email (price must include any quota charge and commission if applicable)?

15. Are you able to be in email contact at least every two - three days to give status reports?

16. Can you visit our website at (YOUR WEBSITE) to get an idea of our line before responding to this inquiry?

Thanks for taking the time out to reply. We are looking forward to your communication.

Best Wishes!

(Your Name)

You can contact me at:

(Your Contact Info Goes Here)

Buy The Fashion Business Center at StartingaClothingLine.com – this sample letter and much more is included in the Pack.

(THIS IS AN EXAMPLE OF JEAN GRADING. DO NOT USE THESE MEASUREMENTS. THEY ARE INCORRECT.)

JEAN PANTS GRADING - UPDATED 10-16-04
METHOD - TOTAL MEASUREMENT OR FLAT
DO NOT FOLLOW THESE MEASUREMENTS - THIS IS ONLY AN EXAMPLE

SIZES	METHOD	1-2	+/-	3-4	+/-	5-6	+/-	sample size 8 7-8
WAISTBAND AT TOP - ROUND MEAS.	ROUND	22	2	24	2	26	2	28
MID HIP (3 1/2 inch below bottom of wb)	ROUND	29 1/2	2 1/4	31 3/4	2 1/4	34	2	36
LOW HIP (6 inch below bottom of wb)	ROUND	31 1/2	2 1/4	33 3/4	2 1/4	36	2	38
INSEAM		32	0	32	0	32	0	32
THIGH -	FLAT	7 3/8	7/8	8 1/4	7/8	9 1/8	7/8	10
KNEE	FLAT	6 3/4	1/4	7	1/4	7 1/4	1/4	7 1/2
LEG OPENING	FLAT	7 1/4	1/4	7 1/2	1/4	7 3/4	1/4	8
FRONT RISE		6 7/8	3/8	7 1/4	3/8	7 5/8	3/8	8
BACK RISE		11 7/8	3/8	12 1/4	3/8	12 5/8	3/8	13
ZIPPER LENGTH:	FLAT	4 1/2	1/4	4 3/4	1/4	5	0	5
FRONT POCKETS:								
OPENING AT TOP FROM OS GOING INWARD:		3 1/2	1/8	3 5/8	1/8	3 3/4	0	3 3/4
LINING HEIGHT:		3 1/4	1/8	3 3/8	1/8	3 1/2	0	3 1/2
LINING WIDTH:		4	1/8	4 1/8	1/8	4 1/4	0	4 1/4
HEIGHT OF OPEING ALONG OUTER SEAM		2 1/4	1/8	2 3/8	1/8	2 1/2	0	2 1/2
BACK POCKETS:								
POCKET HEIGHT AT CENTER		4 1/4	1/8	4 3/8	0	4 3/8	1/8	4 1/2
POCKET HEIGHT ON SIDES		3 1/4	1/8	3 3/8	0	3 3/8	1/8	3 1/2
POCKET WIDTH AT TOP		4 3/4	1/8	4 7/8	0	4 7/8	1/8	5
POCKET WIDTH AT THE BOTTOM		3 3/4	1/8	3 7/8	0	3 7/8	1/8	4

Get spec sheet templates, contracts, purchase order forms & more with The Fashion Business Center at

StartingaClothingLine.com

STYLE BLANK MENS T SPECS - MT 100
XL SAMPLE SIZE. SIZE RANGE: XL - 3XL
DATED: 6 - 10 -04

AREA	INCHES	SAMPLE	NEW SPEC
BODY			
CHEST WIDTH			
CROSS SHOULDER			
BOTTOM WIDTH			
BODY LENGTH			
BODY LENGTH (back side)			
ARM AREA:			
SET IN SLEEVE CONSTRUCTION.			
ARMHOLE HEIGHT			
ARM OPENING			
SLEEVE CUFF HEM HEIGHT			
UPPER ARM SLEEVE LENGTH			
INNER ARM SLEEVE LENGTH			
SHOULDER WIDTH			
NECK AREA:			
FRONT NECK DROP- TOP TO TOP OF RIB			
BACK NECK DROP			
BACK NECK WIDTH - SEAM TO SEAM			
NECK HOLE OPENING			
NECK RIB HEIGHT			
STITCHING METHOD:			
DOUBLE STITCH NECK, ARMHOLE, BOTTOM HEM			
BOTTOM HEM FROM BOTTOM OF SHIRT			
# OF STITCHES PER INCH:			
TAGS AND LABELS:			
MAIN WOVEN LABEL CENTERED IN BACK NECK			
SIZE LABEL NEXT TO MAIN LABEL.			
CARE INSTRUCTIONS, RN# , MADE IN COUNTRY, FABRIC CONTENT ALL ON CARE LABEL.			
CONT: THIS TAG IS LOCATED INSIDE SHIRT ALONG LEFT OUTER SEAM 3 INCHES UP FROM BOTTOM			
CARE INSTRUCTIONS FOR THIS STYLE:			
MACHINE WASH COLD WITH LIKE COLORS, TUMBLE DRY LOW, DO NOT USE BLEACH, DO NOT IRON			
CONT: PRINT			
FABRIC:			
BODY:			
RIB:			
THREAD:			
COLORS:			
COLOR 1:			
BODY: PANTONE #:			
RIB: PANTONE #:			
TRIM: PANTONE #:			
THREAD: PANTONE #:			
EMBROIDERY / SCREENPRINT: PANTONE #:			
SPECIAL INSTRUCTIONS			

Get spec sheet templates, contracts, purchase order forms & more with The Fashion

Business Center at StartingaClothingLine.com

Introduction to Chapter II – Reality of Owning Your Own Line

This chapter was written to inform aspiring designers about the various aspects of owning and operating their own clothing line. There are many problems that will arise in the clothing design business that may not be your fault. But you will have to solve them nonetheless, in the very best way you can. In this guide, we will discuss the types of problems you will encounter. We will also give you many suggestions for solving them.

We had to refrain from mentioning any brand names specifically in this book due to confidentiality. But we will share with you some of the experiences of famous brand designers, as well as experiences of our own. You will be able to learn from the experiences referenced in this book to better prepare yourself for the hurdles of this industry. We are not authors giving you a generalized gloss over of the industry; we actually take you on the front lines of the battle to succeed.

Words from Michael H. on Chapter II

Many people start out wanting to create clothing lines from humble beginnings. Others start out on top of the world like Sean John. No matter where you start, the fundamentals are the same. You must create a good product and sell it at a profit to make it. In this business, sometimes that is easier said than done.

This guide is the first of its kind to give you an in-depth look at the industry before you make huge financial commitments. The knowledge that is shared here will empower you. Nothing about this industry is easy; it is hard work and you have to be willing to do what it takes to make it. Just reading this guide proves you are serious about going after your clothing business dream.

Words from Jay Arrington on Chapter II

Give yourself an Edge

In life as in business, I work to give myself an edge over the competition and situations. My sincere desire is to encourage you to do the same. When we first started in the fashion industry, we strived to learn everything that we could, and to be as knowledgeable as possible.

I think it is safe to say that we've learned a lot, and now this information is being passed on to you. Enjoy it, and make an opportunity for yourself in this $90 billion industry. After all, "You can if you think you can, and if you think you can't, you're right." I read these words one day and they have stuck with me ever since. You can succeed – just think you can! Best of luck to you in your pursuit to be the next hot designer!

Structuring the Proper Team, Part 2

Harmony and Cohesion

A good team is essential to the success of your clothing line. Whether your team is made up of owners, investors or other talented people, it is essential that you have harmony and cohesion. It is essential that you take the needed steps to maintain it.

Certain attributes are paramount to the survival of any company or organization. These attributes are respect, professionalism, and integrity. In order to provide optimal performance, each team member must maintain these characteristics.

Without these three attributes, internal problems could take place and compromise the foundation that you are building upon. For example, if someone on your team takes a leadership position on a project, and the team agrees that he/she is making the right decisions, support should come from the other members of the group.

What I just stated might seem obvious, but, nevertheless, many nascent companies have failed before they could really get started. In plain English, internal arguing among team members slows down or may destroy your progress altogether. If you want to be successful at starting any company, there must be harmony and cohesion among the team members at all times.

Now I'm not saying you should strive to make your company a utopia. In reality your team *will* have disagreements. Nevertheless, there is a way to disagree professionally without caving in your entire company. Unity within the team will be a key to your success and it will be the team's responsibility to maintain it.

One method we use to help maintain unity on our team is called "The We Factor": when the team works as a unit and no longer as a collection of individuals. The language of the team also changes from "I did" to "we did," and every move one person makes for the good of the team is considered a move for us all.

This way of doing business will eliminate finger pointing when a team member makes a blunder or mistake. The team should agree as a whole before any moves are made. It is at this point that a change in language takes place and you begin to say "We" instead of "I."

This industry is full of ups and downs and setbacks, and by the nature of this business you will inherit some of your own. Our aim is to give you as much insight into this industry as possible and prepare you for the road ahead. Since our team has traveled this road before, our hindsight can serve as your foresight.

A very important thing to remember is to always expect the unexpected; unforeseen problems are notorious, relentless and bound to happen. The team's job is to anticipate and try to problem solve any problems before they occur. Remember, anything that can go wrong will go wrong. So whatever task you are performing, ask yourself what can go wrong. Then be prepared if what you imagine actually happens.

There is no I in the word TEAM: **T**ogether **E**veryone **A**chieves **M**ore.

Designing Your Collection

Designing your collections is one of the fun things about this business. For many reasons, you may be actually producing only 25% of the things you really like. There are many different factors causing this. One factor is financing. Your budget – the factory minimums – may only allow you to produce so many styles per month or season.

For example, say you only had $1,000 and one style was costing you $10 apiece. The factory said that you had to order at least 100 per style. You would only be able to produce that one style. To a designer, not being able to bring out all of your designs can be frustrating.

You may find yourself having to alter your designs if you can't fit them into your production schedule when you would like to. You may also find yourself having to change the fabric of certain styles. If your fabric choice is important to the design, then you may have to wait until that season comes back around to make that particular style.

By the time that season comes next year, you have other designs that probably will come before that one. Next thing you know, you may have to totally scrap the original idea or incorporate certain aspects of its design into newer styles.

Another aspect of designing your collection is fabrication and coloring. It is important when you are designing to know what factory is going to make what styles and when. Suppose you have a pair of denim jeans that have suede on them. The suede on the jeans is supposed to match up with the knit sweater being made by a different manufacturer. This is a bad idea.

It is very hard to have two separate manufacturers match up the same color, even if using pantone reference as you learned in Volume I. There was a time we didn't take this into account. That particular order could have turned into a disaster. We received the samples from each manufacturer about a week apart. On paper, the color designs were looking great. However, once we saw the actual samples together, we knew we had a problem. What you have to remember is that many times you don't see what the actual fabric color will be until months into the production phase.

Sure, you will see lab dips, but these don't give you the full understanding as seeing the entire garment in its chosen color does. We had a model try the clothes on and it was terrible. The colors did not match whatsoever. Here is a rule you should always live by: when you are doing a bottom that is supposed to match with a certain top, color for color, make sure the two colors don't touch. There should be a contrasting color separating them.

It is our practice and that of other clothing brands to have multiple manufacturers on the roster. No one relies on just one place to do everything. You have to have back up plans and be well-diversified in your production allocation. Say you are working with just one manufacturer and things go wrong, which they often do for various reasons. Then your designs will have no manufacturing home, and your pipeline is delayed.

The pipeline is an important factor to the clothing entrepreneur. Without a strong pipeline, you will not be able to compete with the competition or keep your cash flowing. The pipeline simply refers to the number of styles you are releasing in sequence (by date).

For an exercise: Go to the mall once a week and count how many times you see something new – something that you didn't see before from a particular brand. How long did it take before you saw those new items? In general, most companies bring out new styles once a month. If you are not bringing out new styles regularly - at least once a month – then your clothing will look old on the rack compared to the just arrived styles from your competitors.

The Pipeline

So when designing, you have to make sure you have strong styling in your pipeline. Each release should be hotter than the last. The last thing you want is your March delivery styles to be hit and miss with buyers after your February styles were too hot to keep on the racks. You have to be consistent in releasing hot styles. You don't want to end up being a one hit wonder.

The next thing about the pipeline depends on your factory. You have to make sure you have your production orders in place to be able to keep your pipeline intact. Once again, this is an area that new designers don't really think about. It has a lot to do with budget forecasting and timing. Timing is one of the most important elements to a clothing line. It is not like selling soap where it doesn't matter if you are late.

Now to further this, let's do a skeleton example of a pipeline plan. Say you have an order of jeans coming in January. You have an order of skirts coming in February. You have an order of jogging suits coming in March. Now, to be able to guarantee that each of these orders arrives on time, you have to do your part.
Your part is either to issue a LC or place a down payment on the order to get it in motion. So, say each of these orders is going to cost $15,000 FOB (FOB term from Volume 1). If you were to sell out of your January order in thirty days, you would have the money you invested in the order back - plus profit - in February.

In order to have a January order in the first place, you would have had to order it the prior October or even September. You would have started your February release in

October or September. Side note: if you are getting your goods made in China, remember the Chinese holiday discussed in Volume 1. We mentioned whole production planning in Volume 1. You ordered your March release in November, your April release in December, your May release in January. By the time you order your June release, you would have the money from your January order back to invest in June's.

If you chose to pay a down payment to your manufacturers, the balance payment to them might not be due until two weeks before they ship your order out. Now if you are having your goods flown by air delivery, then the date of two weeks prior to your January order falls on December 15. If you are using ocean shipping, then you would have had to pay your balance sometime the previous November.

Let's assume that you are paying 50% down on your order when you place it. We also assume in this example that your company's first income is not coming until February. Assume all you have in financial resources at this time is your initial investment money.

- January - $15,000 you have to pay out of your investment.
- February - $15,000 you have to pay out of your investment.
- March - $15,000 you have to pay out of your investment.
- April – $7,500 down payment out of your investment.
- May - $7,500 down payment out of your investment.
- June – you don't have to pay for this order out of your investment money. You could wait until the money comes in from your January order to place a $7,500 (50%) down payment on the order.

In this example, you need a total of $60,000 for your production, in addition to shipping and duty costs. You would not have to pay for shipping cost until the goods arrive at your port. Therefore, in this example you only have to cover your January and February shipping and duty expenses prior to your first profit earnings.

There is a catch, however. If you get this program rolling from the beginning, you will be in somewhat good shape providing you pay everything on time and your manufacturer ships everything on time. The other key point is that you have to sell out before your next production payment is due, or you will have to borrow to cover it.

Donald Trump said that having a hot product may come easy but selling it is the hard part. You have to sell your merchandise for this equation to work. If you don't, your pipeline is in jeopardy. Now what happens when you miss a month in your pipeline from your perspective? One result is that the profits from the current order you have on the table must now fund your expenses and production for the next month. Your financial burden picks up with non-released or late orders.

Example of a well flowing pipeline:

- February you have made $30,000 from your January order
- You have expenditures of $10,000 (salary, loan payments, advertising, office expenses, etc.)
- You put $7,500 on your June down payment
- You pay the shipping for your March or April order depending on your shipping method. Say it is $3,000 for this example.

- You now have $9,500 left and you will be adding your March profits to that.

Example of a poorly flowing pipeline:

- February you have made $30,000 from your January order
- You have expenditures of $10,000 (salary, loan payments, advertising, office expenses, etc.)
- You put $7,500 on your June down payment
- You pay the shipping for your March or April order depending on your shipping method. Say it is $3,000 for this example.
- You now have $9,500 left
- Your March order has been delayed to April because the manufacturer is shipping to you late.
- Now you have to take that $9,500
- Put down $7,500 to keep your pipeline running
- You only have $2,000 left for expenditures and shipping cost of March. You would be $8,000 short in this example.
- What do you do? Borrow? Do you not put down the deposit?
- Your other bills and commitments are due.

Now if you don't sell out within thirty days prior to your next month's delivery, you will run short even more money. If you are running short already and your delivery is late, you could start seeing a month or two go by without a new product in your warehouse.

When the pipeline fails, your designs have to either be altered or cancelled. This is the nature of the beast. You may be thinking, "What if I just try to come out with a new product every other month?" Depending on your overhead and your expansion plan, this will cost just as much money as coming out with something new every month.

The other thing to keep in mind with your designs is that stores like variety. They want to see a big line of clothing. So you as a designer can't go into their showroom with just one pair of jeans and one shirt. The flip side of that is you can go into a retailer meeting with four different styled jeans and four tops and the retailer will just order one style. The business is crazy that way.

The best thing to do is trick them in a sense. You can have a catalog full of different styles. You know that you are only bringing out so many of them; meaning you already placed a factory order for a select few. If they order any style that you aren't bringing out, tell them that particular style has sold out already. This channels them to the styles which you are bringing out. You score points this way because it looks like you are selling out of things. They may even want to order early next time.

If you find that most stores always want the things you aren't bringing out, then you should reconsider how you are deciding what designs to put into production. Remember, this plan will only work if your pipeline is going smoothly and you are delivering to your retailers on time. If you are not, then you have more problems to contend with. Not only will retailers get fed up that they can't get certain styles that they really want, but their second choices are arriving to their stores late.

Aren't these things good to know? You will hear these things only in our book. We will repeat this point throughout the book to help you understand precisely why it was worth your investment to have this guide.

Now on to your truly large companies like Tommy Hilfiger. They order their clothes nine to twelve months in advance of their street date. This means that their designs for 2006 are mostly finished in early 2005. These companies are so large that they have to proceed in this fashion.

You have an advantage because you can get your product to the market faster than the big boys. You can have your hot styles on the market more quickly. And if you are air shipping, you can get them out even faster. You can actually design something today and have it out in 90 to 120 days on average. Use this advantage wisely. Think of it this way. If Tommy forecasted a trend that didn't materialize, they are in trouble. Your ideas, by contrast, should be right on the money because you have the advantage of seeing new trends first hand.

All of this being said, if you were a large brand, you would need quite a bit of money to start up and run your operations. Imagine if your production orders per month were $300,000 or more. Our example above is based on a spending budget of $15,000 a month on production.

Assume you have to order 500 of every style you order. Suppose each pair of jeans you order will cost you $12 FOB and each top will cost $9 FOB.

500 pair of style 1: = $6,000

500 tops of style 1: = $4,500

Your total for this one complete outfit is $10,500.

If you only had $15,000 to put toward production that month then you could not get two outfits. Now if you don't have a separate budget for your shipping and duty, then your $4,500 will be gone as well. Among the 500 that you are ordering, try to get the manufacturer to give you at least two colors, meaning 250 of color 1 and 250 of color 2. Do not be tempted to increase your quantity because you may have $4,500 left if you don't have orders for that additional product. As we talked about in Volume 1, it is better to sell out and not have enough than to have more than enough.

What make designs cost what they do to get produced?

- The amount you order
- The price of the fabric per yard
- Cutting and Sewing
- Dyeing cost
- Washing cost
- Trims
- Packing method

As we all know, the more we buy, the cheaper the price gets. Remember that it is better to have an empty warehouse because you sold out of a product that you paid $5 for rather than a warehouse full of leftover merchandise for which you only paid $3. Getting your money out of excess inventory can be very tough.

The price of the fabric per yard is also a factor in the unit cost of your styles. If you make your goods with cheap fabric then your goods will be cheap goods. Consumers can spot a cheap fabric a mile away. Also note that factories have certain minimums of yardage which they can order or make. This will also determine the number of pieces of a certain style you are required to buy.

Factories in China are very good to suggest using Ramie Denim, for instance. Why is that? We will tell you. Once again, you will only hear this here as we give you the real world insight. Chinese manufacturers will offer you a pair of Ramie Denim jeans for a unit cost of, say, $6. Sounds like a good price, right? Ramie Denim is cheap. If you are making a low cost denim brand then by all means Ramie Denim is for you.

Ramie Denim is a quota-free fabric. Chinese manufacturers try to push this fabric off on new clients because it saves them money and hassle in quota cost and stipulations. We have had a few manufacturers try to sell us on Ramie Denim, but guess what? We turned them down each time. Go out to your local mall and see if any other company in your market is using Ramie Denim. If they are, then by all means join in.

Cutting and sewing is one of the most expensive parts to manufacturing your garments. The more pattern pieces you have in your style, the more it will cost. This is why complicated styles cost more money to make. Make sure that within your market you can get your money out of a complicated style. You have to be able to obtain a reasonable profit margin off of the style. You can get a good mark-up without too much backlash from retailers if you have a hot and in-demand clothing line.

Dyeing also makes up a part of your unit cost. Factories have to dye certain amounts of fabric at one time. It is in your best interest to use **the same fabric in a number of different styles**. Factories will like this as well. This also is a benefit to your collection. Say you want two different styles of tops. Say the factory tells you that you will have to order 500 of each. You could ask the factory if it can produce 250 of each style since both styles use the same fabric. A manufacturer may go for this.

In the reality of selling your product, it is better to have two different styles of tops in the same color than to have just one style top done in two colors. Another thing to keep in mind about dyeing is maintaining color consistency. If you order 500 tops of the same fabric, make sure you tell the factory to order enough fabric plus additional yardage (cover factory mistakes) to make sure they can dye all 500 units at the same time. Fabric in this case would all be of the same dye lot.

One time we ordered 450 dresses. The factory actually screwed up on 125 dresses, so they scrapped them. They then brought in some more fabric to remake the 125 dresses. The problem with this was we had a dress and hat set. When the dresses came in, some were the original color and some were the color of the second dyeing. We had to actually match up the hats and dresses before we shipped them because of the color difference.

Your trim cost is often minimal. Trims are mostly labels and hang tags. The greatest expense in producing trims is setup cost. For instance, you will have to pay a mold charge for each trim you have made. You will be charged for your button designs, rivets, custom zippers, and so on. Most factories will charge you up front for this.

You can opt to have the unit cost per trim included in your FOB cost or you can buy the trims in bulk. It is up to you and your manufacturer. Your reason for paying up front may be to save you money in the long run. You can actually have all or some of the trims shipped to you directly. The trims will come in handy as you can send them to any new manufacturers to be used in your samples.

Sometimes relationships go sour with manufacturers. You may find that you can't get the bulk trims you paid for without other stipulations. In these cases, you will have to invest in mold charges all over again with a new manufacturer. It is good to get any excess trims you paid for sent to you before any full production order is actually done. Of course, leave them with what they need and some excess to cover any mistakes.

Packaging your orders is not that expensive. You basically stipulate how you want your goods packed, as learned in Chapter 1, and go for it.

We will tell you about a story that happened to a company we know. This story will help you understand why you need exposure to the fundamentals of this business before you can be successful. Having hot designs does not guarantee success. There was a guy who was a hell of a designer. He worked for a major brand, designing some of their most signature pieces. For whatever reason, he decided that he wanted to leave the company.

He started his own company a short time later. Now remember, this guy was hot with his designs. Retailers jumped on his product because of the buzz he had coming from this major label. He picked up industry sales representatives because of the hype that pushed his product. Coming out of the gate, his product was initially purchased by over 250 stores. Despite his enviable early success, this man is no longer in business just one and a half years later.

Why is he out of business? Being a good designer doesn't necessarily make you a good business person. Now what exactly happened in this case? This is a lesson to learn from. It involves something we talked about earlier, which is the great big **Pipeline.**

Now as we told you, this man came out of the gate with over 250 stores calling for his product. He only had a certain amount of money to finance his collection for the season. He did not protect his pipeline. Suppose you had $1,000,000 in your bank. You bring out clothes once per season, which is every three months. Retailers bought heavily into this man's season one releases, to the tune of $2,000,000 in sales. To keep things simple, assume his markup is double. That means his production cost on $2,000,000 in sales would be $1,000,000.

These are guaranteed sales. What do you do? Do you realize that you need to split that $1,000,000 into being able to fund at least three seasons (securing your pipeline) and lose money on all of the orders placed with you, or do you strive to accommodate the orders? This man chose to go after his orders. Now what is wrong with this, you might ask? He should be able to use the $2,000,000 he will make to keep things going, right?

This theory did not work for this man and it will not for you either. For those of you looking at this as "I don't have a million to spend anyway," think again. This happens on any scale with this business. The reason why is the amount of time it takes you to get your next product from the sample stage to a finished product in your warehouse.

A number of things went wrong for this person. First, his product did not sell in the stores as everyone thought it would, despite his designs being hot. No one can say what exactly will be a hit with consumers. His product did do well in a lot of stores. But consider this: many of his retail accounts were done on credit.

He shipped his product to stores on January 1. He had ordered the product in September and so spent his whole $1,000,000 dollars in September. He had no money left to spend in October for products which would have come out in February and so on. Now in February, he had less than the $2,000,000 he had sold because some accounts simply did not pay on time or at all. The accounts that did well, meanwhile, were asking him what he had coming out the following month. Nothing at all, he had to respond. His pipeline was empty. As February and March rolled in, his hype had begun to diminish. His accounts had started to move on.

Don't make this mistake. It is better to sell out by not having enough than having too much. Also note the fact that he didn't totally sell out in thirty days or even within that season, which further set him up for doom. Now, let's apply this man's difficult experience to a smaller scale.

When we first started our line, we made this same mistake. We had just run a production run of 250 jogging suits out of China for $38 FOB each. The joggings suits sold out as they were one of the first of their kind. We decided to remix it and release it again because all of the success we had. We found a factory in Korea that could do the jogging suits for $22 but we had to order 750 sets. Selling the remixed suits for the same price meant we could make far more money off the deal.

We timed things so that when we started making money off of the jogging suits, we could pay our final payment to the factory for the next order. Two problems arose. The first one was that the jogging suits were a month late, so we didn't have the money to pay for the next order on time. This delayed the factory in finishing that order. When our new jogging suits did come in, we picked up extra freight cost, as expected. Even though the FOB price was lower, we still paid more in total duty cost because of the quantity.

We had to sell at least 400 suits to break even and pay for the next order. It took us forty-five days to do this and collect our money. This further delayed our next order. By that time, our next order was already two months behind the jogging suits, which meant that all of the other orders in our pipeline were affected. Now if we had just ordered another 250 or even 400 jogging suits at our old cost, we would have sold out and been able to keep things rolling on time.

Time is money. If you try to finance your company with one product of which you order a lot, you will have difficulty in the long run. You have to build slowly, diversify, and grow. Ordering one product in bulk would work if you could have your clothes made and shipped in thirty days. Unfortunately, things don't turn that fast in this industry.

I want to give you one more example to drive this lesson home. Say you invested your whole $25,000 investment in one order because you projected that you could make $75,000 off of it. Say you are selling this to retailers and directly to consumers yourself. First of all, when retailers allocate a certain amount of space in their store for your line, and give you a piece of their budget, it is yours. It is yours until you no longer make them money.

Now if you give them your product in January, they have put your line into their budget. When February comes, you don't have a new product for them. The money they had for you will be spent on someone else's line. What if that someone else sells faster than you? What if your line produced just average sales in their store? They may have been willing to give you another shot in February but you aren't bringing anything out. Now your spot is gone and you will have to re-earn it. This is not always easy.

Now you have your revenue of $75,000 in January and you are in the same position again. Do you invest in one production order or fill your pipeline? Hopefully you know now that your pipeline comes first. For another example, think about the following case. Say you have a $2,000 check that you were going to buy a car with but you just got laid off. That $2,000 will be your last check for three months. Out of that $2,000, you have to pay bills until you go back to work.

By the time you figure out what your monthly overhead is and other expenses, you may find you only have $1,000 or less left for that new car after three months. The same principle applies here. Your $75,000 could erode to $40,000 or less after four months of waiting to get your new order in. This is even assuming that you actually make the full $75,000.

Financing Your Line

Financing your line can be stressful. We covered some ways in Volume 1 to get it done. There is no one way of finding financing. We will not cover traditional bank financing as it doesn't exist too much for the garment design company. As learned in Volume 1, having orders or hot designs doesn't automatically mean that someone will be willing to loan you large sums of money.

As we stated in Volume 1, the best source of financing will begin with you and the assets you can pull together. The next level of financing is seeking small and large investors. Suppose you knew ten people who each could loan you $5,000. Having a great business plan, attractive samples to show, orders, and a great repayment plan may be all you need to land some small to large size capital investors.

Try to pool together as many small investors as you can if you can't find one person with a large amount to invest in you or to borrow from. We use the term investor loosely here. Look at investors as two types. You have your short-term investor and your long term investor. Short-term investors ask for an attractive interest rate for borrowing their money. You may opt to pay them back anywhere from a month to two years later if you set up your agreement that way. Your long term investor may be with you for the life of your company unless you buy them out or they decide they want out.

Picking up long term investors can be good and bad. The good part is it should be a nice boost to your operating capital. You may be able to finance your production and advertising with it. Of course, most investors who invest large amounts will want a percentage of your company. Give them percentages that you are comfortable with based on the amount of their investment.

The thing to keep in mind is that as with most companies, you will have a few rounds of borrowing. For instance, you may start off your company with small borrowed funds to get started. Then you will need to borrow again sometimes to get to the next level. After things are going well, you may have to borrow again to expand your line. Now what would happen if you let somebody buy into your company with $10,000 and you gave them 10% during your first round? Say you had three people like that. That is 30% of your company gone already.

Then in the second round, say you found an investor who has $100,000. Even though $100,000 isn't a lot of money in this industry, say they wanted 20% for their investment. Now you would have 50% of your company gone already and all you have to show for it is $130,000.

If your line begins picking up at a fast pace, you may need to expand beyond the current profits that you are making. Then you would need a third round of borrowing. Keep in mind that most companies have many rounds of borrowing. Now if you bring on one more investor, you should be seeking a minimum of $500,000 or higher at this point. This investor will want a percentage of your company too. What do you do? Well, you could try to buy out the other investors, but this will cost you. Otherwise you stand to lose controlling interest in your company.

Our advice is this: borrow smartly. Your plan should be to go as far as you can on your own workings, as mentioned in Volume 1. Next, you should seek smaller investors to whom you will pay back their money within a specified time period. Smaller investors are people with less than $15,000. Next, you have your $50,000 to $100,000 type investors.

$50,000 can be spent in one month just financing one or two orders or meeting advertising costs. After that $50,000 is gone, you better be selling your merchandise to be able to maintain your company.

So in reality, you should try to come up with at least $100,000 through small investments. If someone did want to invest $100,000 or more, you should think about giving them around 5-15%. Make sure you have planned how to put your investments to efficient use. You should not allocate all of your investment funds at once. You should save some as patch money.

Patch money is funds you can use if your sales are going slow or you have a gap in your pipeline. This is kind of like a nest egg in a sense. They say most businesses fail because they don't have enough capital to make their cash flow smoothly. This is true. This is why we say you need to save a portion of your investment funds to ensure that your cash flow and pipeline stay in good shape. As a rule of thumb, you always want to invest the bulk of your money in what will make you money.

Bringing in large investors is a good thing, but realize that the more people who invest, the more control or input they will want. There is a clothing line that we know of that went to the Magic Tradeshow that had a small booth at first. They later got new financing from a larger (non-apparel) company.

They returned to Magic with a larger booth the following season. They were able to step up their image and also begin doing national advertising. The investor began calling most of the shots. This brand did not take off as the designers or the investor wanted it to. The investor pulled out, leaving the company in a position where they could not go on. In this case, their failure was mostly due to poor advertising and a bad name to begin with, among other things.

The same concept happened with another somewhat famous urban line that had a major rapper attached to it. The designer was able to get financing from a larger clothing brand because the line was doing so well. Once the line stopped performing, the larger clothing brand pulled out, leaving the company high and dry. The larger company did not care about the company attempting to make a comeback.

The moral of this story is once you get a large investor, you better make sure you take your company to the top and stay there. Should that investor pull out, it could mean the end of your company. You would be forced to start over. The problem is that retailers took a chance on you once and they might not be willing to do it again.

Reading this book places you in the position to know what to do with your investments. To be quite honest, you should not start your business officially until you can at least secure $100,000. This means that you should not spend any of your investment money until you have reached this amount. Trying to make a run at it with less than $100,000 is possible but hard.

Keep in mind that the early legwork mentioned in Volume 1, such as getting your office together, securing trademarks, and everything else, should be done out of your pocket or with credit cards. Be creative in how you come up with your financing. Just remember who you get in bed with; bedfellows can be good things, but also very bad things. Make smart moves. Always think of long term objectives. Do not keep your mind in this moment alone. You don't want to end up owing large sums of money to investors that you can't pay back.

Manufacturing

Manufacturing is one of the most complicated pieces of the puzzle. Manufacturing will either make you or break you. There is much to be said in this section. In reality, this is the life or death section of this book. Just as inadequate financing, poor manufacturing will kill your business. Right now you should be extremely glad you purchased this book.

We will start at the beginning. As you learned in Volume 1, there are a lot of people trying to find manufacturers who understand the ins and outs of manufacturing. Some even lack knowledge on specifications. To everyone we state: buyer beware when sourcing your garments to overseas factories!

Before doing business with an overseas manufacturer, put that manufacturer through the initial contact verification check. Check out all of their contact information as learned in Vol. 1. Then begin a series of e-mail trading to get to the bottom of what they can or can't do. Don't be fooled by manufacturers telling you how great they are on quality. Many will tell you about all of these processes for inspection and being ISO 9001 certified. These claims mean absolutely nothing! We have heard and seen it all. The bottom line is you are never really guaranteed quality unless you watch your product being made directly. If you were to spot something wrong, you would tell the manufacturer to fix it right then and there. If you don't have the means to do this, then your chances of receiving the quality you want are **never 100%.** There are times when things will go beautifully and others when your product will resemble the curbside on garbage day.

In this section, we will explore some various quality issues that happened to us and some of our colleagues. Our first production run went pretty well. We worked with a manufacturer out of Hong Kong. At the time, they were doing work for another well-known brand. Hong Kong in general is one of the most expensive countries to do work in except for manufacturing done in Europe. At the same time, Hong Kong gets high marks on quality.

We worked with the Hong Kong manufacturer for about four or five orders. The problem came with our sixth order. Since we had been working with the company for a while, we asked them to help us get a denim maker who could do small quantities. We ordered some men's denim jeans and denim tops. Once manufactured, however, the buttons began to fall off of the pants and tops. How could something as simple as putting on buttons be done wrong? We couldn't blame this whole thing on the Hong Kong business because they had actually sourced our denim program to another company in China. The Hong Kong company was strictly a knit company.

In this particular order, we purchased one garment style top and one garment style jean bottom that both came in three colors. The black color had its share of problems, which was totally unexpected. The denim of the black outfits had a strong smell, like kerosene.

It was terrible. Who would imagine that your garments would not arrive smell free? Really, is that something you should have to worry about? Yes, everything becomes important when you are sourcing your goods from overseas, or from anywhere for that matter. To be honest with you, we probably could write a whole book on overseas manufacturing. You even have to specify with manufacturers that your garments should be free of any soiling or stains.

Anyway, the third problem with this order was the indigo color. We had suede on these garments and if the garments were washed, the indigo would bleed on the suede. The catch to this was we asked the manufacturer to do a dry clean test on the garments before they shipped them. All the tags were dry clean only. Their test came back positive. However, when we put the garments in the cleaners here in the U.S., the garments failed miserably. As a consequence, we had to offer a lot of refunds, credits, and replacement outfits to satisfy customers.

The final blow with this order was that we were forced into producing a color scheme that we really didn't like. The blue and red style we had was one of the weakest colors of the three. We had originally set up to do two different styles that would use the blue and red color. We canceled one of the styles and wanted to take the money from the canceled style and add it to the indigo color. The manufacturer would not let us and somewhat forced us into getting more of the blue and red style.

This was poor planning on our part for changing the styles up in the middle of the order. We were left on the short end of the stick. We had too much of our weakest color. When we sold these items to the stores, the black and the indigo colors sold out which left us with blue and red outfits. It was a blow to our cash flow because now we had a certain amount of dollars we were hoping to make held up in this style.

What you have to remember is that if you are counting on bringing in a certain amount of money from an order and you don't get it, you will have to make cuts in other areas. We next shifted our production to India. We went to India because the U.S. dollar is worth a lot of money there, making their production pretty cheap. Unfortunately, we got what we paid for. India's manufacturing proved to be pretty disappointing. If you look at some well-known labels, you may find some with a "made in India" tag from time to time. However, these tags are found primarily on tops and T-shirts. Don't make denim jeans in India. Trust us.

One of our accounts always talks about another designer who was doing production in India. I remember the store owner said you can't go too far when you have your clothing made in India. I was thinking to myself, "That may be true but we are working with a good guy over there." I was so wrong. When our denim shorts came in, they were the worst. Loose threads were hanging everywhere. The buttons were banged up pretty bad and were not highly polished as they should have been. Sure, we had seen the production samples prior to shipping and honestly they looked good. There are times you will receive a nicely constructed sample and then your production looks like garbage. The grading was even off on this production run. Although there were some good pieces out of this order that we did manage to sell, we couldn't sell them at the price we originally intended. Basically, we are trying to make you aware of different aspects that will need your attention when doing overseas production.

Now, on that same India order the tops had problems. We had a very nice quality T-shirt. In fact, India is known for their great cotton. The fabric was absolutely wonderful. The main problem that affected every piece was that the front neck drop was too low and the width too wide. The larger sizes were affected the most by this problem. The smaller sizes could pass. The other problem was that the printed logo on some shirts was not straight. It was slanted in some cases. Imagine how that looked! Yes, this was truly a bad order.

One of our colleagues at the time moved his production to Pakistan. The prices were good and the manufacturing agent was doing some work for another company he knew. For those of you who don't know what a manufacturing agent is, we will tell you. A manufacturing agent is a middle man between you and the factory. The manufacturing agent will quarterback your deal to manufacturers with whom he or she already has a relationship. This is supposed to guarantee you quality and so on. Agents charge you a fee for their services. Usually this fee is a percentage of each unit price multiplied by the total quantity ordered.

Most of the time the agent fee is already included in your unit cost. We have always paid directly to the agent in these cases. The agent then forwards the money to the factory when it has finished production and done work to meet your standards. A manufacturing agent is supposed to be your safeguard.

This is not always the case, however. Think of this scenario which happened to our colleague's line. A problem arose during the manufacturing of one of our colleague's styles. This style was very important to our colleague's company because he had advertised it everywhere. The buzz for it was crazy. The product was severely delayed. The agent turned out to be a very shady liar.

If an agent or company keeps offering you excuses as to why your product is running late and the delay goes beyond two weeks, know that they are trying to stall you. This agent was saying things like he was waiting on labels to come in from China. Our colleague said I can't wait for that. Do it without those particular labels. The agent would say things like, no you paid me to do a job for you and I want it to be just like you ordered it. At first we thought, "Okay, this guy really cares." Yeah sure he did! This was a stalling technique. If this kind of talk persists in your own agent relations, you will have to perceive the negative pattern and call your agent's bluff.

The next stall technique our agent used was that he claimed that the production had actually finished, but the manufacturer was having problems getting the order on a plane to the U.S.A. He stated that there was severe backlog and delays at the airport. He went on with this lie for three weeks. Can you believe that? Our colleague was calling over there every night trying to figure out what was really going on.

My colleague called in a different freight broker to get the goods out of Pakistan. The new freight broker stated that there was no holdup in shipping out of Pakistan. This was a shocking blow to our colleague. He was furious over the fact that this agent had been lying now for two months. Attempts to get the agent on the phone were proving to be unsuccessful. The agent was avoiding my colleague's calls.

Then the final bomb dropped on this particular order. The agent had finally realized that he could lie no more, as our colleague had now discovered the truth. He apologized and said that he wanted to tell the truth but couldn't let our colleague down.

What actually happened is that the agent, without notice to our colleague, had switched factories from where he normally gets production done. He had never worked with this new factory. Now keep in mind that our colleague had a signed contract with the first factory. Being that our colleague was not informed of the factory change, the new company had no contractual obligations to our colleague to adhere to any delivery or quality standards.

The new factory took their sweet time filling the order. At the same time, the new factory did not really care for the agent. It was a bad situation in which our colleague's company had to pretty much sit back and wait while his extremely advertised style slipped away. This is an extreme case of poor manufacturing but nevertheless we have to include it. You have to be prepared for anything with overseas manufacturers.

A manufacturer delivering your products late is a big problem. The first thing is to make sure you have done your part to ensure that your order gets started on time. If you know you need an order to come out by Christmas, you have to order it no later than August. Next, you need to make sure you are completely satisfied with whatever it is that you are ordering. Last minute changes by you will further delay your order.

Manufacturers hate last minute changes, but it is the way of the business. Don't let them tell you that it is not. We once had a manufacturer tell us that last minute change is somewhat a norm. However, major last minute changes will cost you more money and delay your order. Simple changes can be knocked out sometimes without missing a beat. Keep in mind that some manufacturers may stop working with you if you become notorious for last minute changes on orders.

There was one time when a last minute find in our production sample saved us. We were making some ladies velour jogging sets on this particular order with another company from Korea. We had just received the samples in and the ship date was the next day. As we brought in models to try the clothes on, we noticed there was too much material in the hip area.

It was a huge defect. We immediately got on the phone and e-mailed the manufacturer as well to stop them from sending this order. It is hard to imagine what we would have done with a defective order at that point once it was on U.S. soil. Paying for reworking once the goods arrived in the U.S. would have forced us to sell the items for more than the market would allow. The company ended up reworking the order in Korea because it was their fault. They were still not happy about doing it; they would have rather we hadn't caught their mistake. Where was their so-called quality check at that point?

The bad part is the order was supposed to come in early November but ended up arriving two days before Christmas. The good thing is the order turned out to be very successful for us in terms of the fit and sales. The ladies really loved the jogging set and it sold out in all of our stores. Don't be afraid to stop an order when you find something wrong with it at the last minute. You may lose time, but this is better than losing time *and* money.

After you have ensured that you have done your part to get your order finished on time, it is completely up to the factory from that point. When you place an order with a factory, they will look at where in their production schedule they can fit you in. In general, they try to knock out their most profitable production clients with the big orders first, then squeeze in lower volume orders.

Sometime a manufacturer will give you a completion date without having any real intentions of meeting that delivery date. You will have to stay on the manufacturer and enforce any late penalties that you have agreed upon in your manufacturing agreement. Don't be scared to enforce this contract. You will want to have some of the following things in your contract with your manufacturer:

- If they don't deliver by a certain date, they will be held financially responsible for any changes you have to make to the styles, which could include new fabric, changing the style, etc.
- Your reason for the above stipulation is that you are missing your season and now can't sell the order as is.
- Keep in mind this may further delay your order.

Now the bad part of this is you may get a discount off of your late order but you are the only one who will really suffer, as we mentioned above when discussing the pipeline. Now your January order has turned into your February order. Your February order has turned into your March order. Now you have to review all of your styles and make sure they are still season appropriate for their new dates.

In some cases, you will end up having to alter your styles or cancel them. Meanwhile, your profits are not flowing because of the delay. Your retailers are mad because you aren't delivering on time. As we said, they don't care that the factory made you late; being late only reflects on you and your company in their eyes.

In our beginnings, some five years ago, we were caught up like this. We went to the Magic Tradeshow in Las Vegas and wrote $110,000 in orders. We went to an August show and wrote orders for our immediate items and our future delivery items. We shipped our immediate items but our future delivery items ended up being delayed. Our pipeline was not where it should have been. Why do you think we are strong advocates of the pipeline now?

We wrote $70,000 in future delivery items that never saw the light of day. A delay here, lack of money there, and so on gradually wiped out our paper pipeline. We lost all of those orders for those items. Manufacturing delivery time is critical to your success. It is your job to stay on the manufacturer to make sure they do your order on time. They should be on time with each manufacturing milestone in an order as outlined in Volume I. This will ensure they are at least making progress towards the completion of your order.

In reality, you should make the manufacturer feel that they are lucky to be working with you. You have to possess the power over them. You have to make them do what it is you want them to. They will take advantage of you if you don't. In our early days, we were taken advantage of a lot. We were fortunate enough to keep things going, but it was not easy at that time. We could have easily fallen off our track and failed.

Now back to quality. Quality is the number one reason why you and your manufacturer may part ways. It is a beautiful thing when a sample comes in looking like garbage. You know right then and there that it is time to head for the border. The unfortunate thing is when samples come back looking good. This initial success could just be a front.

Manufacturers know how to trick you. Many of them offer you false promises of world class manufacturing but can't deliver. There was a company we worked with in Bangladesh that sent us beautiful samples and production samples. Based on the production samples, we paid our balance to them and asked them to ship our product. When the product came in, we were totally taken for a long ride. They had changed the fabric on us to a cheaper fabric and our suede trim was definitely not suede. To make matters worse, the grading was so bad that our size ten, twelve, and fourteen all fitted like a size eight. We could not sell this product at all. We had to pull it from all of our catalogs and orders.

It was a disgrace. We had written in our contract with the company that if more than 20% of an order was defective, we should be reimbursed or credited the full FOB value of the order plus any shipping and duty expenses we paid. Guess what? They never paid us a dime. This is an unfortunate part of wire transactions when paying factories. If this had been on a LC (Volume 1), we may have had some real recourse.

The last major thing of this nature to happen to us was when we ordered some different jogging suits out of Korea. A colleague recommended this agent to us. We felt the agent must be pretty good if our friend's company was using her. The bad part is we had a chance to let another company do the manufacturing but chose the Korean woman instead based on our colleague's referral, even though she was $2 higher per unit than this other factory.

The jogging suits were a disaster. The zippers were falling off as soon as you tried to zip them up. This affected about 50% of the order. The grading done on the jackets was off to the point where we had to substitute jacket and pants sizes just to make it work. For instance we had to sell an XL jacket with a large pair of pants, even though it was supposed to be a matching set.

When you are getting your production samples in you need to do the following:

- Request to see each size you ordered
- Request to see each color you ordered
- Make them confirm that the samples are of the actual production
- Inspect them thoroughly
- Make sure the garments are free of strange odors
- Pull on the zippers
- Pull on the buttons
- Wear them to make sure the fit is right
- Measure them to make sure the fit is right
- Put them in the washer, dryer, cleaners or whatever you have on your care label
- Make sure decorative designs aren't crooked on the garment
- Make sure nothing is missing
- Make sure the stitching is straight

- Make sure there are no broken stitches

- Make sure stitching is neat

- Make sure your pockets are deep enough or not too deep

- Make sure your pocket openings are the right size

- Make sure the labels are correct

- Make sure the colors on your hangtags are not bleeding on your garments inside the polybags

- Make sure they are using quality dyes, and that the dyes are fully setting into your garments

As far as measurements are concerned, they must be within the tolerance you specify. The spec handbook we recommended to you in Volume 1 can also be used to calculate an acceptable tolerance for each measurement point.

You will want to do all of these checks to whatever sample you receive from your manufacturers. It is extremely important to do these checks on the production samples. The last thing you need is to get defective garments into your warehouse. These checks do not guarantee that there will not be any bad apples in your mix, but it does give you a little peace of mind.

Now your product is ready to ship. You have set up your dealings with your customs broker and so on. The manufacturer is supposed to send a visa with the shipment to get it cleared once it reaches your country. Make sure they have filled out the visa information correctly before they ship your goods. They must have their garment category numbers correct for your styles (see Volume 1).

We have suffered delays four times over visa issues. Two times, our visa was lost. Once the visa was sent directly with the shipment and then lost by the airlines. The other time we had decided to send the visa by Federal Express to our broker. Even so, the visa arrived very late behind the order. Two other times there were mistakes on the visa.

When a visa is incorrect or lost, you should expect a delay of at least a week before you can get a new one. In the meantime, your goods are sitting in an airport warehouse gaining storage fees. If you want, you could tell them that if the visa is incorrect because of their mistake, they will be responsible for excess storage fees while you are waiting on them to send a new visa.

Next, you have to get your goods through customs. The guys at customs work strictly by the book. They look for any reason to hold up your goods. Most of the time, your broker is your only direct means of communication with customs agents.

We once had a customs agent who wanted to know what method was used to sandblast our jeans. As it turns out, some company has a patented process for doing sandblasting. We had to tell customs that we were not using that particular method. It was quite interesting. At the time of writing this book, who wasn't sandblasting? Is customs asking everybody this question? Who knows?

To close this section, we want to emphasize the following points. Many new designers think that once they have a manufacturer who is willing to work with them, the sky is the limit. Relationships with many manufacturers are like one night stands: it is hard to find a good manufacturer who you can work with for the long term. When you do have one, be sure to do your part to keep your relationship in good standing.

As they say in relationships, the grass is not always greener on the other side. The other point here is to make sure you have the manufacturer sign off on your terms and provisions. Remember from Volume I that even the condition of the boxes they ship your clothes in are fair game.

You have to be the boss. In our company we always assigned one person to be really friendly with them. We had another person who would be on them about everything. It is important to keep that kind of balance. There should be someone taken away by the person who is on them about their screw ups. They have to know that your company means business.

In order for the manufacturer to know this, you have to know how to deal with them. You have to be precise in your decisions and objectives for your brand. You have to know what you are doing. Unfortunately, many times designers run to manufacturers and simply just don't know how things go. Be glad you are reading this book.

Companies like T.J. Maxx and other discount chains buy defective goods and overstocked merchandise from clothing companies all the time. They buy them very cheap, so don't expect to make money there. You may end up only getting $6 or less for a product you invested $12 in. This is why it is very important for you to not over order as well. If you have too much product that you can't move, you may not be able to get the full face value out of it.

You will have to search around through various manufacturers to find one that will make the quantities you are comfortable with. Don't be afraid to be creative in coming up with how you negotiate with them on this. Many factories will tell you off the back that their minimum quantity is one hundred dozen or 1200 pieces per style or more. Some of the larger brands may have minimums of 100,000 pieces per style. If that is something you can do then you are okay. If not, don't be afraid to counter them with what you want to do. It may work sometimes.

You may be able to get a manufacturer, who normally states that their turnaround is ninety days after sample approval, to make your goods in sixty days. Once again, they may say okay but still finish you up in ninety days. These kind of delays are the nature of the beast. Good manufacturing can be achieved. It is not impossible. For every horror story, there are twice as many quality orders being delivered. Just make sure you do your part to ensure that your company gets the best treatment.

Before we leave this section there is one more thing to mention. Make sure your overseas manufacturer is not a sweat shop and does not employ children. You don't want that coming back to haunt you like the Kathy Lee case.

Stay in daily contact with your manufacturer(s). Continually offer your assistants any help they need. Be sure that you believe them to be trustworthy before you begin basing all or part of your pipeline on them. Imagine basing your pipeline on one manufacturer who ends up going astray. Your pipeline would be wiped out while you try to bring someone else up to speed.

It is best to have a different factory working on each delivery. For instance, if you had an order coming out in January, February and March, you should have a separate manufacturer for each of them. Then on your April order, go back to the January factory. This will ensure that your pipeline is protected. Remember these three key points:

- Protect the pipeline
- Protect your quality
- Protect your delivery date

New Safer Way to pay Manufacturers

We discussed earlier in this book about how to wire money to manufacturers if you can't get a LC. Now we want to introduce a new approach that you may want to try. It is a lot safer for you than just wiring money. The solution is Guru.com, a service that lets you the "employer" and your manufacturer "the freelancer" enter into a legal and binding contract. It gives you and your manufacturer that third party oversight. The Guru.com service can be used no matter where you or your manufacturer resides in the world.

Basically, the process works like this. You and your manufacturer create a contract with regards to each order that you both agree on. Then you both go to Guru.com. You can register for free as an employer. Your manufacturer can register for a basic account free, but we suggest you have them register for a Guru Vendor account because the transactions fees will be significantly less. To see what the current price is for your manufacturer to register as a Guru.com Vendor, just click on the "freelancer" link and then click "help." It may also be a good gesture if you pay your manufacturer's registration fee because you are the one who is trying to get them to join this service.

The next thing to do after you both are signed up is: **A.** Post your project / order. **B.** Invite your manufacturer to submit their bid for the order. **C.** You accept their bid. **D.** Your manufacturer uploads the contract you both came up with. Keep in mind that the contract you both agreed to should have also included how, when, milestones, dates, amounts etc. as to how you will pay the manufacturer. You will make sure that you both have agreed to use Guru.com's **safe pay escrow service**. You can contact Guru.com for more detailed information.

Basically, using this service means that you deposit the full or partial amount for the order in the safe pay escrow account. Payments will then be released to the manufacturer based on the terms that you guys come up with. Incorporate the concepts you will learn in this chapter and chapter II -*The Reality of Owning and Operating Your Own Clothing Line* to come up with the best contract. Once you agree to the contract and deposit the funds in the safe pay account, you and your manufacturer will have legally entered into a binding contract. Both of you must perform according to the terms of the contract. This way you are safe to get your order the way you specify and your manufacturer is guaranteed they will get paid for the order if they deliver it the way you want. This is why this new method is something like an LC without going through the hassle of dealing with a bank.

You now have a third party making sure your project goes as planned. Everyone wins! Keep in mind that you may end up paying a little more for your order if your manufacturer chooses to pass on some of the Guru.com's cost per transaction over to you. Transaction cost will be around 5-12% overall. However, we feel that it will be in your best interest to utilize this service. Plus, Guru.com offers unbiased arbitration services to both parties should a dispute arise, which is why they charge the transaction fees. You never know if a dispute will arise.

Also note that you can put money in your safe pay escrow account to pay for your orders using credit cards, bank accounts, wires etc. In addition, note that many top companies use Guru.com, such as Johnson & Johnson, Motorola, Hewlett-Packard and more. Please take this advice and do some more investigation on Guru.com and how it can help you. If you decide to use their service, please keep us updated on how it is working for you. E-mail us at support@startingaclothingline.com.

The Inside Story on Dealing with Retailers

Selling to retailers in most cases is the life line of your company. Without proper distribution, clothing companies would not have an outlet to sell their merchandise. Sure, there are web sales, but they are a fraction of what takes place in the physical world. Most people would rather try their clothes on in stores before purchasing them over the internet.

With this being the case, you need retailers. In our sales guide we went into the basic dealings with retailers. In this book we will actually take you inside selling to retailers. We will give you some different cases to learn from. Knowing these things will better prepare you to make sound moves when selling your line to retailers.

The first thing we want to touch upon is something we mentioned in Volume 1 and the Sales Guide. Do not give credit to a retailer if your factor will not. I remember when we first had the thought to get a factor, we were very excited! We saw getting a factor as a way to increase the likelihood that a store would order from us. Everyone likes credit right? A retailer wouldn't mind having thirty days go by before they have to pay you. In that amount of time they could have sold your merchandise and let it pay for itself. The problem is, though, most of your mom and pop type stores don't have good credit. I recall when we got our first round of orders from Magic. We submitted all of the retailers' names and orders to our factor. Out of forty stores, only three of them were approved for credit.

Some of these stores we thought were doing pretty well. But looks are deceiving. This business is based on image. You can look flawless on the outside but your inner workings may be deteriorating. The funny thing is some of these retailers who were not approved insisted that other factors were giving them credit. They may even insist something is wrong with your factor.

For the most part, these are retailers who are paying COD for their orders but are trying to get over on you. We believe COD to be the best payment method if done correctly. Note: you should never accept a company or personal check for payment despite the store owner telling you their checks are good. Don't let a store owner talk you into accepting these forms of payment. Yes, it might be inconvenient for them to get a money order but it will be even more inconvenient for you to monitor your collections efforts on their account.

There was a store that at one point convinced the Fed Ex driver, whom we would later report, to let him pay for our order with a company check. Our accounting staff was upset when a company check appeared. It just so happened that in this case the check cleared our bank with no problem. That is one of the few times, however, when personal or company checks that we've received haven't bounced.

We had a store in Louisiana that was very successful. All of the hot brands were retailed from this store. Before we knew exactly how to structure the COD forms, this guy had sent us our first lesson. He paid with a company check. It bounced. He requested us to redeposit it on a certain date. It bounced again. We sent him to collections because months went by with no cash from this man, though he continued to claim that he would take care of his costs.

Another guy in Pennsylvania had a similar story. He had actually been approved by the factor for $1,000 on net thirty. However, our first order with him totaled $2,000. In being new, we decided to give him the credit ourselves since he was approved by the factor for the full amount of the order. He actually sold out of our order within two weeks and wanted to reorder.

We were excited but at the same time we asked him to go ahead and pay for this second order COD and include the payment for the first order. It totaled up to be $3800.00. This happened at the same time as the other bad COD order. We did not put the proper COD secure funds labels on the package. He paid with a company check.

His check bounced. We had to send him to collections. His store would later file for bankruptcy. This guy actually had a history of preying upon new lines. He was notorious for writing bad checks for clothing. He tried to come off as a nice big shot in the industry. He would basically use the sales from new lines to pay for his other existing lines.

The moral of this story is: you are the new guy with an unproven track record and others will take advantage of your position. Say a retailer sells $500 worth of your clothes and none of his Tommy Hilfiger. The bill arrives. He may choose to pay Hilfiger over your account even though it was you who made him the money. This is very sad but it happens. The same thing can be said of COD.

Retailers sometimes have many COD orders coming in on the same day or week. Based on their funds that day or week, they may opt to pay for their most profitable lines first. Yours, in this case, may not be one of them as you are new. The unfortunate thing is sometimes your package is returned to you.

Returned packages cost you money. In our beginnings, we incurred huge Fed Ex bills. The money it was costing to bring samples from overseas was expensive. We were getting in samples almost every day. Each box would cost anywhere from $75 - $180. Then we were trying to get our money as fast as we could so we were shipping to some of our retailers using three-day express instead of ground transportation.

The reason we worked this way was for cash flow purposes. Let us break it down for you because unless you have been doing it, you will not know. Here is the general cycle.

Cash Flow In the Apparel Industry by Average Number of Days.

Start Order Downpayment	Finish Production Pay Balance	Ship Goods Air	Ship Goods Ocean	Clear Customs	Time to ship goods into your warehouse	You ship to Retailers	COD delivery to you	Bank Clear Money Order
	60	7	40	4	1	5	7	5

Total Time by Air:	89
Total Time by Ocean:	122

Looking at the numbers above gives you a general idea about how things go. We will come back to this chart in the cash flow section. Right now we just want to bring your attention to the time it takes for you to ship to retailers and actually get your money order cleared at the bank.

We were sending packages to retailers three-day express because the COD check would come back the next business day. We wanted our money fast. So if a retailer would get their order the day it arrived at their store, we would have our check the next day. This cut our time by eight days. Eight days may not seem like a lot but when you have other orders in your pipeline where the balances must be paid, eight days can be plenty.

The other way we tried to save time was to give discounts to retailers who paid by postal money order. Postal money orders clear the bank the same day, so you save four days on bank clearing. This is good for us as clothing companies but retailers hate going to the post office to get a money order.

That year we spent over $40,000 with Fed Ex. We learned a lesson from this. Often times we found that some retailers did not have the money to cover our orders the first time we sent them. They would then request that we resend the orders. Most of them would get the orders on the second attempt, but some still didn't get them. It is these type of retailers that you have to look out for.

The ones who eventually pay for the order have to pay for the first delivery as well. The ones who don't pay at all leave you having to cover that cost. Keep in mind that we were not actually charging retailers full shipping cost because we were shipping three day express. Do not ship in any form but ground is our advice. Think profits over a few days saved in delivering and processing time.

We basically were throwing money down the drain in an attempt to better our order start to payment time. This one company we know of had it very bad. They had over 200 stores at one point. Many of their retailers did not pay them whether it was COD or factored money. The clothing line went out of business, owing over $200,000 to their factor and $30,000 to their freight carrier.

In this business, there will be times when you are left holding the shipping bag. It happens. The key is to not ship someone the second time without requiring that they pay up front. We had also started a plan where they would have to go get a money order first and fax us a copy of it before we shipped them. When your line is in-demand you are in a better position to make retailers play by your rules.

Here are some of the typical excuses retailers give as to why they didn't get your package when it was initially delivered:

- They weren't at the store when it came
- They came too early
- They came too late
- They didn't have time to go out and get the money order
- They couldn't leave the store to go get the money order
- They didn't have it at the time because they got so many other COD orders that day or week
- They say things have been slow
- Can you resend it on this date?
- They had the wrong amount made out
- They simply forgot

The funny thing about sending COD is this. You always want to call and verify with the store right before you ship their order. You want to tell them the amount and what day it will most likely reach their store. They will say, "Okay, send the order." If you're dealing with an unreliable vendor, four days later the package is coming back to you with one of the excuses above. It's like, "Hey, we just talked to you four days ago and you said you were ready to get it."

This business is crazy like that sometimes. It happens to all clothing companies that send COD orders. This is one reason we stopped doing COD to mail order customers. We started making them pay up front before we shipped them. The worst thing is when your carrier commits the error of not enforcing the secure funds payment guarantee and a company check slips in. This has happened to us four times costing us $5,000 in lost sales. Make sure that you insure your packages for more than the $100 that is provided automatically.

If your carrier makes a mistake like that and the retailer gets your merchandise with a bogus check, you can hold your carrier responsible. When sending COD, here are some of the actions you should take:

- Confirm the amount with the retailer before sending.
- Give them a heads up as to when they should expect the package.
- Make sure you have designated secure funds payments on the labeling. Confirm with your carrier that you are doing it right to avoid mistakes.
- Send your packages using ground services (no overnights unless the retailer prepaid or paid you with a credit card).
- Track your shipments everyday over the internet.
- If you see "recipient not available or funds not ready" on a return slip, call that particular retailer to see what the problem is.

In general things go smoothly with retailers. If a retailer gets by without paying you, sometimes you will not be able to collect his or her money. Collection agencies are a joke unfortunately. We have sent many stores to collections over non-payment. We have never gotten a dime unless the store really wanted to pay us. Most of the time, you will just end up writing it off on your taxes as a bad debt.

Another potential problem happens when the retailer doesn't pay the factor. The factor has already advanced you most of the money on the sale. Depending on your arrangement with the factor, the factor could force you to repay the amount he or she advanced you. You may find that the payment you were counting on coming in from another company has now been pulled back in by the factor to cover the other guy who defaulted on his payment to you.

Another thing you want to make sure of is that when your retailers pay the factor, they indicate that the payment is for your company. There was a time when the factor credited one of our payments to another clothing company. Then the factor told us we had committed fraud because the retailer paid us directly and he had paid us as well for the same order. The factor withheld a $1200 payment to us to cover the advance.

We knew we hadn't committed any fraud. We called the retailer and they stated they had paid the factor. They provided us with the check number and we called the factor. The factor found out it was his error. So we asked, "Where is our money that you guys are holding?" Unfortunately for us, our factor was on his way out of business and took our $1200 right along with him. The lesson here is to verify and stay on top of everything. There are many potential problems in this business. You must keep everything documented.

The real issue in terms of dealing with retailers is your company's positioning. If your company is strong and in-demand, retailers are more likely to take care of you. You have to do what it takes to make your line hot. If the people are demanding your line, then retailers will have to play fair with you in most cases. Just selling out in their store a few times does not guarantee they won't ever jerk you around with payments.

Department Stores

Most of this discussion has been geared toward your smaller non-chain retailers. Dealing with chains and department stores is another thing. It is every designer's dream to be sold in department stores. You should be at the top of your game before entering into such deals when they present themselves. You only get one opportunity. Make it count.

Before presenting your line to department store buyers, you should make sure you are doing these things:

- You are shipping on time (at least eight consecutive months of on time shipping).
- Your pipeline is running smoothly.
- You have forecasted your styles to the point where you know what you are bringing out nine to twelve months from now.

- You are confident based on your delivery track record that each style will be coming out.
- Your advertising and marketing has created a significant demand for your products.
- Your profit margins on each unit sold are adequate.
- You have a track record of quality manufacturing.
- You have great fitting clothes.
- You have a factor.

If you are just starting out, chances are you don't yet have all of these things under your belt. You need all of these items in place. **<u>ALL!</u>** You do not want to get into a department store and be right back out of the door because you rushed in. Positioning is everything in this business. If you are not positioned correctly, you will suffer various consequences.

We have seen many lines come into department stores and leave right back out with the next season. Even celebrity lines aren't exempt from this painful treatment. Department stores give you a certain amount of space and that space is supposed to make a certain amount of money. If your clothing is not selling at a good rate or at all, your merchandise will be returned to you.

Unlike with mom and pop stores, which have to keep your merchandise after they pay, department stores operate totally differently. They will charge the clothing back to you, or deeply discount their payments to you, if everything is not sold. We know of one lady's line where the department store discounted her clothing to the point where she made no money at all. Also note that typically department stores want anywhere from net 60 – 120 days.

Now is it really worth being in Macy's if you are actually losing money? If you believe this business is about ego you should think again. This industry is about your bottom line. If you make 500 outfits and gave 250 of them to Macy's where you weren't making any money, you will go out of business sooner or later if you persist with this logic.

The bottom line is you have to be able to generate demand. **He who has the people has the power.** It is a battle for respect in this business no matter what size of retailer you are dealing with.

Another thing to note is department stores are cut throats on your unit prices. They will always demand that you sell your product to them at a certain price. This price may be lower than your budget can take. Of course, if your line is in demand you will have more leverage when negotiating prices with department stores.

There is the belief that you can make it up in quantity. That is true if you are doing a lot of quantity. If you are not, then this theory will not help you. Now if you are producing 100,000 plus of each of your designs then this may work for you. If you are doing 1,000 of each style, however, under pricing your merchandise will send you packing your bags very quickly.

Your business practices must be up to par. Your quality has to be on point. You have got to separate your company from the many other lines on the market. Many designers think that you achieve this through creating different designs. The way you run your business is just as important as your designs. You have to be firm in your beliefs and terms. A compromise here and there may be necessary but don't make it a norm if it will jeopardize your company.

Magic Tradeshow

Dealing with retailers at tradeshows like the Magic is tricky. As we told you in our other two books, most new lines are desperate to get orders. In reality, you should be concerned with who you sell your brand to. You don't want someone posing to have a store who is really selling out of her basement or trunk.

Larger clothing companies require buyers to present a certain amount of information to be able to even see the line let alone carry them. Non-desperate brands strictly enforce many of the following requirements:

- Store has been in business for at least one year
- Require a financial statement
- Must be approved by the factor if they don't do COD
- Must have pictures of their store inside and out
- Must carry other similar brands in their store
- Can't carry knock-offs
- May send a representative to inspect the store
- Must order certain minimums
- Must be a certain distance from another retailer selling their clothing already
- Require a deposit down to open the account

Desperate new lines at Magic don't care about half of these things. They will write up and order for anybody that wants to write. Many times they end up with bogus orders because of this. Just as there are many want-to-be clothing lines, there are want-to-be retailers. It must be one of your practices to require each new account to put down a shipping deposit.

You should save this money and use it for that purpose only. The best way is to just keep it filed. Then every time you ship them, they pay for the shipping with the incoming order. If a time ever arises where they don't accept their order, you can then deduct the shipping charges from their deposit. This way you will never get stuck holding the shipping bag. You would be surprised at how many stores order items that they don't accept once the items reach their door.

To a certain extent, taking deposits at Magic also locks a retailer into carrying your line. Deposits also show you that a retailer is serious. The key thing in this is that you only want to use their money in this case. If a store decides they don't want to work with you and want their deposit back, you should have it available to give to them minus any shipping fees charged to them.

You will get many valuable contacts from the show such as manufacturers, factors, and models. The models come in handy sometimes when you may need one of them to start working for you on the spot.

Another aspect of Magic is about how much you should be spending. A lot of new companies go to Magic and overspend easily. I recall our second time going to Magic. We decided to take eight models from our home city, plus our sales staff and company owners. We paid for the models' hotel rooms, plane tickets and daily expenses.

There is an agency that works with Magic that can supply you with Las Vegas models, but they are rather expensive. Usually, there are plenty of models just walking around who will model for your company on the spot if you pay them. The other thing you can do is to just use mannequins. We found that a mix of mannequins and real models was the best selling mechanism.

The last thing to mention about Magic is that your booth location is everything. You want to be located in main aisle ways where there is a lot of foot traffic. You also want to be located next to other hot brands. The best way to ensure you get a good location is to tell Magic organizers who you would like to be next to. The other thing is you have to pay them as early as possible as booth spaces generally go to those who pay first.

Sales Reps

Sales Reps are an important part of your business. You cannot be everywhere at one time, so you need people out there whose only concern is to sell your clothing. Many new designers turn to reps who are selling for other lines to help get them in the door in many places. These type of reps are expensive as we mentioned in our other two books.

Industry sales reps don't take on new lines for the most part. Selling to retailers, who have trust in them, is their bread and butter. If they sell your unproven line in all of their retail connections and you don't come through, it will damage their credibility. Their credibly is far more important to them than picking up your line, even if you have a hot design.

We hear reps talk all the time about this company and that company. It is quite interesting hearing about the business through the eyes of a clothing rep. They have their own ideas about how to be successful in this industry. We have had the pleasure to experience life from all points of view, which is what makes us experts on this subject.

One rep told us how he sold a new line to all of these retailers and the clothing company could not deliver. The orders were late, and sometimes they didn't come at all. This line had a celebrity face to it, which is why the rep took the line in the first place. The rep lost a few of his key accounts because he carried a line that didn't perform. Stores hold grudges when they lose money.

In our beginnings, we approached a rep who was writing millions of dollars in orders for a major label. He was very impressed with our designs. He felt we were very original and would go far in the business. He said that he would not even consider representing our line until we had three successful seasons of on-time shipping, quality products, and in-your-face advertising under our belt.

He said he would check with our retailers to see how we were doing with those things. There was another rep who was only concerned with how much extensive advertising we would be doing. He wanted to see our financial statements and our design forecast. Reps don't play around when it comes to picking up a new line.

There are others who will say they'll take your line on for a certain price. They may carry your line along with them but may not push your line as much as their other lines. In order for your sales rep to push your line, you have to be positioned right as we mentioned earlier. If your line is weak in terms of lack of demand, no one will respect it, even if you are paying them. Of course you can follow the advice we mentioned in Volume I on getting a rep; that may prove beneficial to you. Even with that approach, you still need a hot line to truly jump off in the retail world.

Another aspect of the sales rep segment of your company is fair treatment. We have heard countless stories of reps leaving a company because they felt unappreciated. A good rep should make good money. It is that simple. If you do not pay your reps for a good performance, the next guy will.

You also have to make sure that you are paying your rep's commission off of the top. As human beings we tend to want to do things by the book, but in reality often waver. Say you just cashed a check for $5,000. Your rep's commission is $1,000 of that amount. Your rent at your warehouse is due and for this example say it is $5,000. You aren't expecting any extra cash into your company for three and a half more weeks.

The warehouse rental office will not tolerate any more late payments from you. Many companies have chosen to pay the rent first. What if you make this decision and in three and a half weeks you don't get the amount of money you were planning on. There are reps who have left companies because the company owes them a considerable amount of money. You have to take care of your sales team. Make sure that you figure their commissions properly. You don't want to short them, or overpay them for that matter.

Being a traveling sales rep is a hard job. Traveling reps are away from their families selling your product. They have to believe in your product to be good at selling your product. If they sense a weakness on the end of your company, it will reflect in their presentation. If they are carrying more than one line, they may not end up showing yours at all to a buyer. Good sales people can get your business off to a great start providing you have all of your business in order.

There are reps that can become your company nightmare as well. These reps will take your company to the bank without producing a dime in sales. We had this one rep who wrote only one order in his whole three month stay with us. Get this. The one order he wrote turned out to be a bogus order from his brother who had a fake store. His credentials had checked out but I guess we didn't investigate him thoroughly enough. In this business make it a point to investigate to the utmost anyone or any company you will be doing business with. Don't just trust them on the strength of what they are saying.

We told this rep that we would cover his daily expenses at Magic only if he produced sales. He had this big book of retailers that he was saying he invited to come to our booth. None of his so called appointments showed up that week. He blamed it on our booth location.

The bottom line is he was a joke and we fired him right there at Magic. We wanted him to return our samples to us after the show. So what he did was send them to us COD for the $700 he claimed we owed him from coming to Magic. Needless to say, he became the proud owner of those samples.

In closing, make sure you and your sales team are prepared when dealing with retailers big and small. From our sales guide, which gives you the basics, to this book, which gives you the behind the scenes footage, you should be ready to tackle this task. Remember, retailers are the life line of your company. Their success or failure is your success or failure.

Opening Your Own Store(s)

Having your own store is expensive but may be necessary. A prime example of why owning your own store may become inevitable is the experience of Tommy Hilfiger. Tommy Hilfiger opened twenty-nine new stores in 2004. While their wholesale profits were down in 2004, their sales direct from their own stores were producing great numbers.

Opening your own store – or stores - allows you to be less dependent upon other retailers. Many designers have found opening their own store to be truly beneficial and rewarding. The bottom line is this: when you sell directly to the consumer, you will make four times your investment. For example:

- Say you paid $10 for something.
- You wholesale it for $20.
- The store then sells it to their customer for $42.
- You too would be selling your clothing for $42 from your own store.
- You will make $32 on the sale while the retail store only makes $22.

If you sell half the amount of your produced goods from your store and half from retailers, you can expect to have higher profits. It is because of this that you may be able to sell your product for less than you really want or need just to make sure your wholesale prices are market friendly.

You definitely want to sell your merchandise for the price you are requiring other retailers to. If you don't, they will not carry your line. Why would customers buy it from them when they can get it from you cheaper? In addition, you should open an internet store without even thinking twice about it. We have sold to customers from all over the world from our website. Note, however, that internet sales cannot solely support your company. Look at internet sales as a supplement.

Competition

No matter how you look at it, you are competing with other clothing lines. You may think you have no competition because you have the hottest designs out, but that will not be the case. You are competing for your brand's place in the mind of the consumer. You are competing with other lines for a piece of your retailer's budget. You will have to earn your success, beyond just producing a hot design.

Advertising, Sales and Marketing

Until you are a famous brand, the primary goal of your advertising should be to make money. Establishing brand awareness remains secondary. For the most part, your advertising should channel consumers to a certain product you are selling. The key theme of your advertising is a product you are actually selling.

You do not want to advertise something that the people cannot buy. This will not help your bottom line or make your precious advertising dollars make sense. Don't be scared to call off an ad or push it back if your product gets delayed or canceled.

You also want to make sure you are advertising with companies that are connecting with your target market. There are plenty of places to advertise, so make sure you choose them wisely.

Being a new clothing company, you are sometimes faced with a dilemma. Should you concentrate your advertising and marketing efforts regionally or nationally? Regionally is a great idea if you didn't have other factors to consider. The primary determining factor for aiming regionally or nationally is, almost always, how much product **you have to order** from the factory.

The more accounts you have, the better your chances will be of selling out. You can't control where people like your product. You may find that your retailers are spread out all over the country. Your advertising efforts would have to aim nationally in this case. This doesn't mean you shouldn't engage in some locally driven promotions where your accounts are located.

When you mention the word national, there is a cost involved.

With that in mind, don't spend too many dollars on local advertising that is too expensive. We have seen some locally produced magazines that cost almost as much as some of the national publications. You will have to figure out the most cost efficient way for you to reach your target market.

Remember this story as well. There was a company that started out after we did. They advertised in all of the major magazines for eight months before they even brought their first product out. What new designers don't realize is that your first ads are the most important. People are drawn to new lines and want to be the first to sell and wear them after seeing your print ad. However, they will want exactly what they see in the ad.

In our very first national ad, we didn't have anything in the ad in production or in our warehouse. We got an overwhelming amount of calls for our ad items, which we had printed up for image branding with no real intention to sell. This was a huge mistake. As you know now, the amount of time it takes to get your product made and to the stores is pretty long. By the time we thought about actually producing the styles we had advertised, the buzz that the ads had generated was gone. Let the big guys build image and brand awareness. You focus on selling your product. Remember this advice: a print ad is like a catalog page with a message.

Back to the clothing company we mentioned. They advertised like crazy all over the place. Most of their advertising didn't make sense, though. There were times when the owner of the line even had himself in the pictures with the other models. What were they selling? Another thing to note is the fact that they went out of business owing a lot of money to various magazines who had given them credit.

This is why we warned in Volume 1 to accept credit with caution. Make sure you get the most out of your advertising dollars. We have cancelled free ads just because a product we wanted to advertise was going to be late. Don't take credit terms on an ad thinking you will be able to sell enough merchandise from the hype of the ad to cover the cost.

Now the line we mentioned actually got picked up in over 200 stores based on their advertising. They did well in half of their accounts, while the other half struggled to sell their product. Their catalog of unfocused ads had failed to generate the demand in their target market that would lead them into supporting the line. Many stores stopped ordering from them. Others didn't pay their outstanding invoices with them.

The retail backlash from their clothing not selling ended their business. Advertising alone can only get you so far.

Fashion Shows: to do or not to do?

Fashion shows – a night of glamour or a waste of money? In this section we'll examine both scenarios to present you with the proper insight into the world of catwalks, models, and so-called exposure. A fashion show is a collection of designers showcasing their designs for the upcoming season.

Traditionally, the designers are not charged a fee for their participation in these shows; however, these designers are well known to attract public interest. In your local areas there may be a fee for you to exhibit your line in a show; however, you should use good judgment when deciding which shows to participate in. In retrospect, it's safe to say that we misapplied a sizeable amount of dollars on the runway. Fortunately, for you these guides have been written to stop you from making similar mistakes. Lucky you!

Ok, quick question, if an invitation is extended to you to showcase your clothing line in a fashion show, should you have to pay? Well it depends on many factors. Below we name a few:

- Who are the main attractions featured in the show?
- Are there any fees involved?
- By participating, will your sales increase?
- Will you gain real exposure for your line?
- How much advertising and marketing will be done for the show?
- Will your line be mentioned in the advertising of the show?

These are some of the things to consider when you are thinking about participating in a fashion show.

The main objective for being in business is to make money. If a promoter wants you to pay a fee to partake in his fashion show, you might want to consider not doing it, unless your line stands to really benefit. For example, if a fashion show is going to be held in your local area with established brands showcasing their lines for the upcoming season, you might want to be involved, even if there is a fee. Associating with success is smart.

The reason why is because by placing your line among well-known brands you give off the image of stability while promoting brand awareness. Now here is where things get tricky. The fee could cost you anywhere from $1,000 to $2,500. You will have to decide if your company will benefit from exhibiting at such a fashion show. In my opinion, you might want to participate once or twice for the experience and opportunity to present your line with the big boys. This could also be good for your brand's image!

Okay, have you heard the old saying "If it doesn't make dollars, it doesn't make (cents) sense"? Well, that's not just a cliché; in business it is a fact. When it comes to doing fashion shows, you have to be careful not to channel too much of your investment funds in that direction. In life, we are all in search of balance: balance in our families, careers, love life, and spirituality. Why should the fashion industry be exempt from that divine process?

The point I'm making here is when you pour your hard earned money into some other person's venture, be sure that it's going to balance out for your benefit. So in conclusion, our team learned to intelligently appropriate our dollars. Instead of a fashion show to gain exposure, we started investing in the service of public relation firms or other more efficient means to gain better exposure.

The proper channeling of funds is critical in the beginning stages of your company. Be careful not to expend too much money on fashion shows. At best, a fashion show provides only one night of glamour.

Photo Shoots

Another aspect of creating your advertising and marketing campaign stems from great **photo shoots.** A good photo shoot is the result of a well-planned story board to convey your campaign's message.

In our beginning stages, we had some quite interesting photo shoots. One of our first photo shoots was for a national magazine. We were very excited. We had a few models show up for the shoot along with make-up people, a stylist and a few spectators. We were doing the photo shoot inside of the photographer's studio. It was our first experience with a photo shoot, so things were quite interesting.

The male models were too busy flirting with the female models. Some of the female models had brought their boyfriends, who didn't want their girlfriends posing certain ways. The make-up artist made up one person in a way we didn't like. The photographer didn't really have a good vision of what to do. The experience became somewhat chaotic. Yet all of these things were our fault and could have been avoided.

There were some good photos that came out of the shoot. We would have hoped so after spending a total of $2,000 on the photo shoot, which is cheap by many standards. A top notch photographer can cost you that amount alone. Remember, the best photographers do cost money and you get what you pay for. Just to let you know as well, we had used a mixture of professional models and amateurs in this shoot.

What exactly is a professional model? A professional model is someone who has been trained to model and has modeling experience. To have a successful photo shoot, there are certain things that must be adhered to. Sure, photo shoots should be fun but there is a limit to the play. If you are doing a photo shoot, you should make sure of the following:

- No boyfriends, girlfriends, or friends of any kind on the set
- All models must arrive on time or be docked, or not used
- All models and photographers must sign releases
- Keep other spectators off of the set (even your own friends)
- Give the make-up people a clear description of how to make up each person
- Don't be afraid to tell the make-up artist to redo someone's makeup if you aren't satisfied
- Make sure the clothes you are taking are in good condition
- Make sure you have a clear idea of the kind of shots you need for your campaign, e.g., a well planned storyboard
- Make sure your photographer is using good film
- Make sure you or anyone else isn't flirting with the models
- Keep things professional during the shoot

- Male and female models aren't allowed to trade phone numbers during the photo shoot
- Everyone knows in advance what they are getting paid
- Everyone has a clear idea on how you will use the pictures
- Models know that you may or may not use their picture after the shoot
- Models should be told in advance if you want them to bring or wear anything special to the shoot.

Doing the above things can lead to a successful photo shoot, which can lead to a great campaign.

Public Relations – Your PR Strategy

The very best thing for your line will be hiring a PR firm. A good public relations strategy is very important to the new clothing line. PR. Take a good look at those two letters because you are going to want and need to see more of them. PR is going to be more of a friend to you than advertising will ever be. Why? Because it can serve you well. Advertising is what you are trying to say about yourself; PR is what others are saying about you. For example, if you tell someone that you make the best chicken in town, they may or may not believe you.

Now imagine if a third party told someone that you make the best chicken in town. That person would be more likely to believe a third party than you. This is called third party confirmation. What others are saying about you carries more weight than what you say about yourself. In reference to your clothing line, get others to talk about your garments, and the public will believe it! That is what PR is all about.

It will be up to you to decide what message your line will convey. What is the content of your line? What is the definition that will define the meaning of your line? How will you be different or separate from others? These are questions that only you can answer, and whatever those answers are, PR will be the best medium to speak to the consumer with. In closing, publicity can be free or it will come with a price. You can save money by doing the leg work yourself or hire a firm to develop a PR campaign for you.

The Cash Flow of a Clothing Company

Here again is a graph of the typical cash flow.

Cash Flow In the Apparel Industry by Average Number of Days.

Start Order Downpayment	Finish Production Pay Balance	Ship Goods Air	Ship Goods Ocean	Clear Customs	Time to ship goods into your warehouse	You ship to Retailers	COD delivery to you	Bank Clear Money Order
	60	7	40	4	1	5	7	5

Total Time by Air: 89
Total Time by Ocean: 122

In the above example, you see that the total number of days from putting a down payment on your order to actually having funds available in your bank account is around 122 (ocean shipping).

Another thing to keep in mind is that sometimes shipments are late, as we mentioned, which could add ten to twenty days more on top of this. Our current record for the latest production order was 120 days. This is standard for some larger manufacturers, but not for us. There is always the potential for things to go wrong somewhere in this timeline.

Many times retailers will ask you to ship their goods on a certain day, which may be a few days after you get the orders. You are ready to ship them as soon as you get them to start making money. Then you have the retailers that you ship to that don't pay the COD when the order gets there.

You have all of these potential delays at your door. The other side of this is the excess inventory you ordered that doesn't have a name on it just yet. You will be trying to find retail homes for those excess items. All these things have the potential to push back your income on this order. You can go from 122 days reaping the financial benefits of the order to 152 days or more easily.

This is why we told you in the beginning that securing your pipeline is critical. If you were to do one big order and then try to fund future orders off of the big order, you would not be ordering your new product for at least 140 days. Then it would be another 140 days or so before you earn money off of that order. You have basically wasted a whole year on two orders if this is your plan.

The toughest part of your clothing business will be getting your pipeline and cash flow to run like a well-oiled machine. It is in this stage that the most capital is needed. Once you have your cash flow turning, you just have to make sure your product is selling.

Many designers plan what they will bring out by what they want to see come out in a particular season. This is fine to do. The ultimate approval will be made by your budget, however. The budget may say you can only do three styles instead of the seven that you wanted to.

At the end of every month, you want to make sure you have a positive cash flow. Adding on styles to any given month will depend on this number. A successful clothing line should always have a healthy cash flow at the end of every month. You never want to have your budget so tight that if things go wrong you get in financial trouble. In terms of forecasting on your income statement, you will have to be realistic. Donald Trump once said that even the best laid plans don't always go accordingly.

If your cash flow at the end of a month is negative, you will have to backtrack through your pipeline and either raise prices, trim expenses, adjust quantities or cut styles. This may also be a sign that you are trying to do too much. The larger your cash flow is at the end of the month the better. It will shield your company from slow sales and other difficulties that may arise.

Your basic income statement (used for projections) should include these items:

<u>Month</u>

- **Sales Income**

    Direct Sales via your website and/or store

    Wholesale segment direct by you

    Wholesale segment by sales reps (subject to commission)

- Cost of Goods Sold (includes)

    Down payment on next order

    Balance to be paid on your incoming order

    Shipping Cost of your incoming order

    Estimated Duty cost of incoming order

- Gross Net Profit

- Total Expenses

    Advertising

    Sales Rep Commission

    Website

    Loans

    Employees/Salaries

Supplies

Samples

Shipping and Mailing

Rent

Utilities

- Net Income for the month
- Cash Flow Balance + / - at the end of the month

Your beginning cash flow at the beginning of the month is whatever you had left over from the previous month. To get your new balance, you add your net profit or loss from the current month to the cash flow.

Your cash flow is the most important aspect of your company. It ties right in with your pipeline. If your pipeline struggles and you fail to add to your cash flow every month, your cash flow will start to dwindle. This will make it hard for you to keep your projected pace. You may find yourself having to borrow money to keep things going as you would like. Borrowing will not ultimately solve your problem. Your problem is that your sales are not being generated to the extent that you need.

If you do not correct the problem you will find yourself in debt. The bottom line is you have to sell whatever you order. You have to be profitable to stay alive. Your goal should be to sell out of every order in thirty days or less. To do this you will need to have your incoming order already pre-sold.

Do not get caught up in the belief that you can borrow your way through anything. Borrowing is a temporary fix. There will come a day when you can't borrow any more. Do not let your company get in this position. This is why we advocate that you have a strong sales plan and well-forecasted pipeline.

Sometimes you don't know what will be a hit with consumers and what will not, and retailers can be fickle. Your business is at the mercy of other people. You are depending on your supplier to ship on time. You are depending on them to ship you quality. You are depending on retailers to order your products. You are depending on consumers to support your products.

I want to touch on another quick subject just for your reference. When you are planning out your pipeline, you will want to be kind of lean on your January and June delivery months. These are slow months in this industry. There is not a lot of wholesale buying going on, so you don't want to order too much merchandise in these months or you may not be able to sell it all within thirty days.

Please understand that you have to perform. You may have looked at your company as a design company. That is the wrong outlook. Instead, think of yourself as a Fortune 500 company. You have to perform financially to stay afloat. You will have to make key financial decisions to make sure your business will be able to grow and expand. Just as many companies have gone out of business because they aren't selling; there are those that fold because they mistakenly tried to accommodate a huge demand.

If you can't service all of your accounts, then you should raise your retail order minimums and cut the weaker stores. It really makes no sense to go out of business trying to do something you probably can't do anyway. Say overnight you find yourself with a $1,000,000 in orders for one month's release. To produce the goods to support $1,000,000 in sales may cost you around $500,000.

Say you only have $200,000 available in your pipeline to cover four months of releases. This would break down to basically $50,000 a month. You are $450,000 short of being able to meet the $1,000,000 demand. Don't do what others have done. Don't take your whole $200,000 and let it ride on this one big order. We talked about this in the beginning of this book in the pipeline section. Be modest and take things slowly.

You are the master of your clothing company. It is you alone who dictates what you do. There is no law that states you have to service all of those orders if you can't do it in a healthy way. If you have a large investor who wants to back these orders, then by all means go for it. If you don't, you will have to go to a select distribution channel. Only the hottest stores which are ordering the most will have your products.

You can add on stores as your cash flow grows. It is that simple. Sure you will lose some of the stores that wanted to order your goods. They may get mad and never want to order from you again. Which would you rather have – a few stores mad at you or your company going out of business? The fact remains that for those who take this risk, putting all of their money on the big order, will find themselves caught up. This has happened to a large brand that we know of. The brand was sold everywhere as there was a significant demand for it.

You have to pace yourself correctly and let your business grow. Do not be afraid to turn down orders. There are so many people who don't believe in this logic, especially people who know nothing about the industry. You have to be smart. Are you just here to be a one hit wonder or are you here to have long-term success? You will have to be the one to decide.

Clothing Industry Myths

To succeed in this business you first have to get some myths out of your head. The top ten clothing industry myths are:

1. Finding a manufacturer automatically means you will succeed.

2. Banks will loan you money just because you have a great business plan and orders.

3. A larger company will come to your rescue and offer you a distribution deal.

4. A good name automatically means success.

5. Having a booth at Magic guarantees that the buyers will come to your door to order.

6. Advertising automatically translates into sales.

7. Celebrity endorsements automatically bring you sales.

8. Most manufacturers do quality work.

9. A production deal will present itself if you get a lot of orders.

10. Having a lot of money behind you guarantees success.

Don't get us wrong, these things have the potential to help you along. It is the decisions you make around these advantages that will make you or break you.

The Top 11 Factors that Determine Success

1. Efficient use of financial assets and planning

2. Selling out of each order within thirty days at least 85% of the time

3. Quality Manufacturing and Merchandise

4. On time shipping of a well-planned pipeline

5. Support from retailers and consumers

6. A great pricing structure on your products

7. A strong team dedicated to the success of the company

8. Hot designs

9. A good image and brand awareness

10. A great advertising and public relations plan

11. Great customer service

Successful lines are the ones that adapt to changes in the environment. You have to constantly reinvent your company to stay fresh in the consumer's mind. You have to think like a champion. You cannot underestimate your competition. You have to be able to think outside of the box and come up with creative ways to move your company forward.

What worked for another company may not work for your company. Fubu was able to achieve success due to the use of LL Cool J, but for the most part this is not reality any more for upcoming lines. There are exceptions of course, but they are few.

You have to be quick on your feet to overcome obstacles. You must think with a business mind instead of a designer's mind. Having a clothing company is a business while being a designer is a skill and a gift. Just because you are a designer doesn't make you a good business person. This book helps you make that leap – from designer to business man or woman. Just think, can a trained doctor necessarily possess the know-how to start and operate a whole hospital?

There are days when you may fail at something. You have to get right back up and keep running the race to make your company successful.

With All of These Potential Problems – Why Do We Do It?

The apparel industry is a $90 billion per year problematic industry. Things are always going wrong. The days where things go according to plan are very limited. Yet it is those days that make everything worthwhile. There is nothing quite like selling out of an order and having stores call us to order more.

There have been few things more satisfying than seeing samples come in for the first time and having them be a true reflection of our vision. We still get excited whenever we see other people wear our clothes no matter who they are. We love when a customer calls in and tells us how much they love our clothes they just ordered.

We love seeing our clothes come down the runway and hearing people clapping and congratulating us. Photo shoots and ads coming alive are also awesome. Traveling and meeting new people all around the world are beautiful things. We love seeing the write-ups on our garments in magazines.

The personal financial benefits you can reap from running a successful clothing line can be substantial. The status, fame and recognition you may receive from having a hot line will make you proud. There is no feeling better than people appreciating your creativity. This is why we do what we do. These will become your reasons for persevering as well.

When the good things happen, it makes all of the sleepless nights worthwhile. It is this passion that keeps us going even in the midst of darkness for day will soon come and all the goodness thereof. Let this book help you on your path. Formulate your own plan of action using this book as a general outline for success. We wish you the very best in your endeavors.

"To achieve success you must first make a passionate effort and work at it with diligence and conviction!"

-- Michael H.

Introduction to Chapter III – Selling Your Line to Retailers

Having retail locations for your product is one of the most important aspects of your clothing business. Without the proper retail action, your company will find it very hard to succeed in this industry. This guide has been written to educate fashion entrepreneurs on the various aspects of selling a clothing line to retailers. Aspiring designers need to know how to deal with retailers prior to approaching them. This guide will give you the insight and confidence you need to be able to present your line to retailers. Just by reading this guide, you prove that you are willing to command your share of this $90 billion per year industry. A good sales plan is essential for success. Be sure to read our additional guides as well to give you the full resources needed to be successful in this competitive industry.

Getting Your Sales Plan Together

You must have your overall plan together before approaching retailers. Some key decisions have to be made. If you are reading this book, you obviously have some interest in selling to retailers. We will begin on this point. When selling to retailers, it is important that you first decide who your likely retail customer is and who your target market is. Answering these questions will allow you to begin your sales program. You must know what stores to approach and why. You must know the answers to some key questions before they are asked. Let us begin!

Who Is Your Target Customer?

Who is your target customer? The answer to this question will tell you what stores to approach. There are three customer types in general. One is your trendsetter who will buy a new line that meets his/her taste just to be different. A second customer type is the trend follower who mostly buys established brands that everyone else is wearing. The third customer type is a blend of the two. In general, there are more type two (trend followers) in the world. Now why is knowing this important?

Knowing what customer type your clothing appeals to should affect what stores you want to pick up your line. Some stores cater to each of these customer types. Department stores and chain retailers cater to trend followers. Your average store caters to these same customers as well. Some boutiques cater to the type one customer and a certain percentage of the type three customer. Being a new brand, your customer type is mostly that of the trendsetter. If you have a good advertising / marketing plan in effect, then you could begin to pick up, slowly but surely, the trend-follower customer-type as well.

Trend followers in general look to national magazines, actors, and musical artists to see what everybody else is wearing. This type of customer does not believe in taking fashion risks. They, in general, play it safe. They want to wear something that is recognizable to their peers. Wearing something established in this sense gives them status. Remember, this is the largest customer base, and so your overall goals should lead you toward this customer type if you want to mass distribute your line. If you are designing one of a kind and limited released lines, then you must start targeting boutiques that cater to the trendsetter type of customer.

What Type Of Clothes Do You Sell?

Retailers will ask you what type of clothing you sell. This question is important because there are many types of retailers. Here are some of the types of retailers out there (Note: Some involve combinations of these areas):

- Men's Wear
- Ladies' Wear
- Missy
- Juniors
- Children's Wear
- Infants
- Jeans
- Dresses
- Coats
- Leather
- Swim Wear
- Casual Wear
- Suits
- Accessories
- After 7
- Athletic Wear

- Shoes
- Discount

If you are reading this guide, you probably have decided what your area of interest is. Now you must look for retailers that sell the type of goods that you are designing. You do not want to be caught trying to sell men's jeans to a women's only boutique. To avoid this possibility, do a little research by either calling the store or visiting them on the internet if they have a website. Simply ask the store what brands they carry and what type of clothes they sell. If they are located in your city, a trip to their store is recommended.

How Long Have You Been in Business?

How long have you been in business? Retailers will ask this for a number of reasons. They first ask just for general knowledge. Then they evaluate your answer the following way. If you have not been in business very long, these first three things will come to mind for the retailer:

- How is their quality if they are just starting?
- Will they ship on time?
- Will my customers take to their brand?

They may not relay these questions to you, but they will be thinking about them. If you have been in business for a couple of years and they have not heard of you, then they will wonder why they have not.

It is up to you to answer the "How long have you been in business?" question. You could choose to use a number of different start dates. You could set your starting date to when you actually registered your trademark, or even the first date you shipped to stores. You do not have to lie, but pick a date that makes sense.

In What City Is Your Company Based?

Retailers will ask you this question for a number of reasons. Often they will seek to use this information while they are selling your merchandise. They will tell customers where your line is based. Many times consumers like to purchase items that are not made in their city unless they are in LA or New York (fashion capitals). The main thing here is that if you are selling your merchandise in stores within your city, make sure the retailer has an understanding of how to sell your items.

The last thing you want is retailers telling your customers that you are a local designer or company. In general, many consumers do not like the concept of local talent. You may ask why this is. While some customers love to support local companies, others do not see wearing a locally made garment as being cool. Furthermore, you do not want your line to seem like charity. Retailers encouraging buyers to purchase this product because it is based right here in our city sounds like charity.

You want your clothes to sell because the customer likes them, not out of support. Also, in your beginning stages, you may seek to sell directly to consumers yourself with this approach if you looking to generate capital. When we were starting out, we did not take this approach. We simply wanted consumers to buy because they liked our products.

Even now, some of our hometown customers still do not know we are from the same city. As a designer, you want people to wear your clothing because they like it, not out of charity.

Retailers also use this information to decide how good your fashions will be. With New York and LA being the fashion capitals, retailers assume that companies from those cities will have nice fashions. The good news is that many new and respected fashion companies are springing up all over the country. As they say, it is not where you are from but where you are at.

Why Do You Think a Particular Store Will Be a Good Place to Sell Your Line?

This question is very important for you and the retailer. You have to know why having your line in that particular store will work. First, you should want to sell your clothing around similar brands. A similar brand simply means that both of you have approximately the same price points and status. An example: you design upscale jeans that cost the consumer $100. You will want to sell your clothing in a store that carries, for example, Seven Jeans (Retail around $100 +). You would not want to sell your jeans to a store where the highest price jean is $29. Your jeans would not sell in that type of environment. It will also play on the image of your company. Consumers will wonder why an upscale jeans company is selling their jeans in a discount jean store. Conversely, the retailer selling $29 jeans would not buy your jeans anyway.

You also want to make sure the store you are selling in is not selling knock-offs. In this case, you may think you are selling beside similar brands, but really you are not. You can get an idea if they are selling knockoffs by doing a little pricing research. Start by investigating the brands in the store; check the price tags of known high end or moderate garments. See if the price is where you normally would see it; if not, then it might be a knock-off.

Now back to why your goods will sell in their store. You can use a number of approaches. Having a plan A and a plan B is a good idea. Now let's say you have a retailer that carries only established brands. From your earlier thoughts, you know that the majority of your customers will be trendsetters and type three consumers. You will want to pitch your line by saying they may need to offer an alternative to people who want something different. You will have to convince the owner why your line fills that void.

Now approaching boutiques that already cater to your customer type will be a little easier, but you still will have to convince the store why it should give your line a shot. Why will customers want to buy your product?

In order to win the boutique owners over, they have to see your niche. What are you doing to make your company **unique**? What is that extra touch that will make consumers lean towards your product? The key point is that you have to design differently. You have to let consumers see your creativity. If your clothing looks like everything else, then what would make customers buy your product? Designing clothes that look like other brands will cause you to lose your trend-setting customer as well.

Keep in mind that we are not advocating outrageous designs, but we are saying you should be unique and a have a niche. As we stated in our Volume 1 guide, being different is easy. The real goal is to be different and hot at the same time. Achieving this balance will give you the edge for both wholesaling and retailing your product.

What Are Your Price Points?

This question is one of the first to come out of your retailer's mouth. Retailers are concerned with what they have to pay you and what consumers will pay. In general, there are three pricing categories: high-end, moderate, and low end (discount).

Some department stores cater to all of these categories. Most small retailers and boutiques, however, try to stick to one category. The trend is changing somewhat: some retailers are seeking to have something for everyone to keep their profits rolling.

Retailers will next get into the price points for specific categories. Now in moderate pricing, you have jean retail prices between $50 and $125. Retail price is mostly figured by key stoning. **Key stoning** is simply doubling the wholesale price paid for a style. Then $2 is added to get the retail price. So a $72 pair of jeans can be assumed to have cost the retailer somewhere around $35 or less.

Therefore, when the retailer asks you, for instance, what are your price points on your jeans, your reply will be around $34 wholesale, $72 retail.

There is a catch. There are average wholesale prices in each category. Large, established brands set the lead in this area. Let us say that your Tommy Hilfiger Jean is selling at a wholesale cost of $32 a jean. You come in trying to sell your jean to that retailer for $38. They are going to tell you your price point is too high because you are new and their customers may not have heard of you.

You will either have to come down on your prices, convince them why your jeans are worth the extra money, and/or have advertising out to back your price up. Just think if you owned a store. Say you have an extra $300 to spend. Say you buy 30 pair of PEPE jeans per month for $32 each, and you sell out repeatedly. Would you rather buy more PEPE jeans or spend $38 on an unproven brand? In general, the market works this way, but there are always exceptions.

Possibly, you can get that retailer to allocate some dollars your way. You will have to give a compelling argument. Even if your price is the same as Hilfiger and PEPE, you will still have to tell the retailer why he/she should have your brand in the store. Having a price point similar to other brands is half the battle.

So what have we learned so far? What is that secret key to success? Being different but hot at the same time with a good price point can spell success.

Where Do You Advertise?

Where you advertise is an important consideration. Retailers will want to know. If they see you will be advertising in national magazines and around their city, they are more likely to give your line a shot. It is important for them to know their customers will be able to identify with your brand. As mentioned earlier, the majority of people in this world are trend followers, and so most stores cater to this customer type.

Advertising in the right places will allow you access to these customers. Remember, he who has the customer behind him has the power. If you have a strong customer following, as well as customers seeking your products because they've seen your ads, then a retailer will be more willing to carry your brand. Your advertising should reflect your company's image and price points. A luxury looking ad will tell consumers that you are high-end, if that is your market.

Retailers also ask this question to see if you will be in any magazines that they have heard of. I remember when we were first selling our line to retailers, we would name a bunch of unknown magazines. The first thing a retailer would say is "Never heard of it." Then the next thing they would say is "Most of my customers read things like *Vibe*, and the *Source*." *Vibe* and the *Source* are widely distributed magazines.

A side note: do not put too much money into unknown or local magazines unless they make you an offer you cannot refuse. The national magazines are all the retailers want to hear about if you are using this in your sales pitch. We got wise to this fact and began advertising in national magazines. It made a big difference.

How Will You Bring Buyers to Their Store?

Do not make the mistake of thinking once you sell your product to a store that your job is done. Thinking this way will cost you in the end. Getting your products inside stores is only half the battle. Now you and the store have to be concerned with making sure your product moves out of that store. If it does not, you will not be getting any new orders from this retailer.

The funny thing is that some stores will be able to move your product with no help while others will struggle to move it. In general, you should have a marketing plan in place to approach them all the same way.

Your first goal is to figure out ways to get traffic to their stores to see your product. You could use various promotions and contests to draw traffic. You could have someone in that area passing out postcards with their store listed on them. Advice: You can have one standard postcard and use stickers placed on them with this information (money saving tip).

Next you need a plan to get them to buy once they are inside the stores. Point-of-Purchase advertising comes into play. Retailers will want posters and postcards to convey your product's image to their consumers. Visit some of the retailers in your area to see what other brands are doing to help you come up with your ideas for point-of-purchase displays.

Who Else Carries Your Line in Their Area?

Retailers will ask this for a number of reasons. Initially, they will want to know if another hot store in their city has it. Let us say the hottest store in that particular city is carrying your line, then they will want to jump on it too because the line must be hot. That is their perception at this point. If you land the hottest store first, then it will pave the way for all the others. This is a good thought; however, getting that account is the hardest.

The other way is to go from the bottom up. Get the lower people first and then news of your line doing good will make its way up to the hottest store, which may then want to do business with you. If you do not have any retailers in their area, then retailer may think the following:

- They want to be first and exclusive with your line.
- They want to wait to see who else picks you up before they give you a shot.

Retailers that want to be the first ones to carry a new line represent your trendsetter type buyers. They want to get in early on your line. Retailers that want to wait to see who else will carry your line first are followers. When a retailer asks you to be exclusive with your line, a few key points come into play.

First, you must know your sales plan for a certain area prior to approaching stores in that area. You have to know how many retailers are in that area and how large the customer base is. In general, nothing is wrong with selling your product to only one store in a certain mall or one store in a 4-mile radius.

This strategy cuts down on pricing wars where your retail price keeps getting lower, which will reflect badly on your overall image. Having space between your retailers allows them to sell your product comfortably. Sometimes retailers do not want to carry your line if many other stores will have it unless you are extremely hot. If you are not and if too many stores have your brand, retailers will wonder if you will create enough consumer demand for all the stores in the area. No one wants to be left with product.

You can sell to more than one store in a certain area if one store was doing all women's clothing and the other was doing men's clothing. The other thing to keep in mind is how big of an order the store wants to do to be exclusive. If they are not ordering a lot and someone else comes along who wants to order more, you may want to switch ships.

Retailers will try to get friendly with you or your sales rep so that you will not pull out on them if you get hot and they are not ordering as they should. If this kind of situation arises, after you have told a retailer they were going to be exclusive, first try to get them to raise their ordering level. You also should consider how long you have been working with this retailer and if they have been giving you steady business.

Do not rush to the new person who claims he will buy bigger quantities than so and so if you put your line in their store. We have seen this strategy backfire. It will be hard to go back to that loyal store to ask for a second chance. Remember, your job is to build solid stores.

What Is Your Return Policy?

Retailers want to know your return policy for obvious reasons. They just want to make sure that you stand by your products. They want to know that you accept a return if something is wrong with their order. They want to know if the order is short that you will send them whatever is missing.

In general, you want to make sure they notify you as soon as possible about any problems with the merchandise that could include quality issues or missing items. Be ready to help!

How Do Your Clothes Fit?

Retailers want to know how your clothes will fit their customers. They will often tell you how their customers like their clothes to fit and what is selling the best in their store. They will ask you if your garments fit a particular way. They will use this information to decide whether they want to carry your line. They will want to know your size range as well.

It is your responsibility to sell them on fit. If you know you have great fitting clothes, make sure they know! It is your job to send out catalogs and promos with models wearing your clothing to demonstrate your fit. The key point here is that fit is important! What is the size range of the items you offer? Make sure you have a good size range for your market.

Do a little research by going to a few stores and looking at some similar brands in your market. What sizes are they selling or not selling? If your retailer thinks that a certain size range in your market is being overlooked, then you could add those sizes as well to your size range. This will add to your niche.

Are There Any Celebrities That Own / Design or Are Endorsing Your Line?

Retailers ask this question to see how much hype is behind your line. If you have celebrities on your team, feel extra free to mention it. If you do not, you can still make it. It is hard to get celebrities these days as they have become quite expensive or are in the middle of launching their own lines. Remember that having a celebrity behind something does not guarantee success. Plenty of celebrity lines have fallen by the wayside. If you have worked for another clothing company, you will want to bring this up. Make it sound good but truthful at the same time.

Do You Factor / Who Is Your Factor?

Retailers want to know if you factor. For those of you who do not know the term, here is a quick definition. **A factor** is a bank that buys your invoices from you at a fee. The factoring process typically works like this:

- You ship goods to the store that was approved by the factor.

- The factor pays you around 80% of the total amount of that invoice within a day or two of the retailer receiving the order.

- The store then has to pay the bank instead of you, usually within 30 days.

- After the store pays the bank, the factor will give you the balance 20% minus their fee, which is typically around 3-5%.

Now, we will get into the implications of this question. Retailers will have these thoughts in mind:

- Do you use a factor that they have credit with?

- It gives your company credibility.

- They can try your line out with no up front cost because they do not have to pay until 30 days after getting your merchandise.

- If they do not have good credit, they will wonder if you do COD.

Whatever payment terms you are offering, make them aware of them. If you factor, let them know. If you can only accept COD, let them know. Remember the other items mentioned on this subject from Volume I and Volume II.

What Are Your Minimums?

Retailers want to know what your minimums are. Minimums simply mean what is the least amount that they have to buy of one style or per order. They want to know how much they will have to risk by carrying your line. In general, the lower your minimums the better, unless your products have a low price point. Most established clothing brands have minimums that are ½ dozen per style on to a dozen per style. It is up to you whether you want to go lower than that with your minimums.

Some companies tell retailers that they have to order a certain dollar amount on each order as well. Once again, this is totally up to you. Just starting out, you will want to make it easy for retailers to pick up your line. You cannot be too hard in this area. Remember, if your product does well in their store, they will reorder from you. The next order could be larger than the first and so on.

Do Your Clothes Come Pre-packed or Open Stock?

Retailers want to know if your clothes come pre-packed or open stock. In general, we have seen retailers want it both ways. Pre-packed simply means, for example:

- They have to buy six pieces of the same style;
- You have six pieces of various sizes already grouped together;
- You spread those six pieces into various size combinations;
- Say you had men's jeans from size 30 – 36,
  you would have a pre-pack with one of each size in it;
- The retailers have no choice in this case;
- They must get one of each size or whatever size breakdown you choose to have in your pre-pack.

Many retailers do not like being forced into getting certain sizes that they might not be able to sell in their store. You like pre-packs because they are already packed and allow for fast shipping. Open stock means that they can order in any combinations that they want. If they wanted to get six pieces of one size, they have the right to do so.

The key here is to give them the best of both worlds. Tell them it is open stock. If they do not order different sizes across the board or are slow to tell you, it is best if you offer them a size combination that your other retailers are doing (pre-pack). More than likely, they will opt to go with your suggestion.

Do You Give Discounts?

Retailers want to know if you give any type of discounts. Once again, this is totally up to you. You could give them a discount if they order over a certain amount from you. You could give them a discount on reorders. Really, you have control in this area. You sometimes will have to choose between your bottom line and getting that account. Just make sure at the end of the day you are accomplishing both. See Volume I and II for more info in the area of achieving the right profit margin.

Another time you may want to consider a discount is if something was wrong with their order. This is after the fact, however; yet it is still good customer service.

Do Your Clothes Come Pre-priced and with Hangtags?

It is important to send your clothes to retailers pre-tagged. You will want to have your suggested retail price on the clothes. Consumers like that because they feel the store is not trying to cheat them. We know of a store where customers constantly complain because none of the clothes has price tags. If your retailer is taking the tags off, now that is another thing. You will want to make sure that your clothes are ready to be sold once they hit the store and that all size/price tags are visible to the customer.

Do You Ship on Time?

This question is not only important when you first present your line to a retailer, but it is important every day of your business. If you do not ship on time, you will lose retail customers! Not shipping on time is one of the main reasons retailers will close an account. When you are trying to get a sales rep, they will want to know about your shipping as well.

A sales rep will check around to see what your shipping habits are. Treat shipping on time as a priority! If you tell a customer that their product will arrive in a **delivery window** between January 1st and 31st, it had better be there. Do not come talking about shipping it to them February 26. They will cancel the order in some cases. If the pattern continues, they will stop working with you all together.

We know of many companies that were not able to deliver on time, and it cost each one of them. Of course, delivering late may not be your fault. It may be totally the fault of the manufacturer, but to the retailer, it is your fault. They do not have to see the manufacturer, nor do they care why shipments were late.

Another important aspect to delivering on time is keeping new products coming (your pipeline). You will want to have your deliveries of new styles set up for at least every one to two months. Most lines bring out new items once or twice a month. You will want to ship items in groups to keep shipping costs down for you and the retailer.

Customer Service

You should make it a point to have excellent customer service. Customer service is not to be talked about but to be lived. You should seek to make your customers happy whether they are retailers or the end-customer. Happy customers come back to buy. You cannot successfully build your company with customers defecting. This does not mean be a push over if a retailer tries to take advantage of you. It simply means do your best to keep your customers so that you can build instead of rebuild.

This completes this section on getting your sales plan together and knowing the questions before they are asked.

Finding the Right Stores

There are books available with retailer listings. One such book can be purchased from our website:

- http://startingaclothingline.com/html/books.html

Other ways of finding retailer listings include:

- Your yellow pages;

- Typing in a brand name (+ retailers) to see what comes up (Internet search);

- Looking in magazines;

- Listening to the radio for new store openings.

You should be looking for online stores as well as physical stores. If you are seeking to sell your line in department stores, you can look in the retailer listings book above or simply do the research by calling that store. Then ask to be directed to the buyer for your market.

Once again, it is important that when you do find stores you make sure you guys are a perfect fit for each other. Thousands and thousands of stores are out there. Make sure you do not over sell your line as well. Have a realistic number of stores that you can accommodate. Set goals as to the number of stores you want to service in a given year.

Sales Reps

Having a sale's rep(s) to get orders is a good thing, but finding industry sales reps is difficult. Most sales reps will not take on your project because you are too new. If you have any of the following, such as major funding, contacts, celebrity endorsements, and a great advertising campaign under way, you may be able to score an industry vet. The good thing about industry vets is that they have a network of retail contacts to launch your product easily in some cases.

You can still find and approach some of them by doing a little research. Look through local clothing tradeshow books or visit trade shows to look for them. Be watchful for the sales reps that will take you to the bank whether they get you orders or not. In this book, we will give you some suggestions on how to find and train non-established industry reps to sell for you in the apparel industry. Many times, this will be your best bet for creating your sales force.

Here are the best ways to find sales candidates for your line:
- Your E-mail lists;
- Job posting sites on the internet;
- Family and friends in other cities;
- Job postings in newspaper employment sections; and
- Referrals from customers.

Asking your customers, E-mail list, family and friends if they know of someone who might be interested in selling your line *is a good idea because of the energy.* These individuals are already excited about your product. They believed in it enough to have bought some, and so, therefore, they will carry that same energy into selling your line for you. This is **the new way of the future**. You heard it here first; in fact, we created this concept in the fashion industry.

The art of selling to retailers is changing. The old conventional ways of selling clothing lines are dying out. Now think of it this way. The average industry vet will charge you a weekly draw + commissions. We once had a rep who wanted to charge $4,500 a month draw + expenses + 8% commission when we were starting. We did not have that kind of cash, especially since he mentioned that he wanted the first three months paid in advance!

Sure, he stated he had contacts to over 100 stores from his current job selling for another large line. We almost considered it, but later both parties would decide to call the deal off for various reasons. What would make reps cost that much? Well, you are paying them that much because they have retailers who will more than likely give your line a try based on the rep's record of accomplishment. They also will be traveling across a certain territory (usually multi-states) with your line.

Established clothing industry sales reps will ask you some of following questions:

- How long have you been in business?
- Whom do you sell to now (name stores)?
- Where are you advertising?
- How much money did you make last year and so far this year?

- Do you ship on time?

- How often do you come out with new products?

- Where is your clothing made?

- Who is endorsing your line?

- What are your projections for next year?

- Can we see your financial statements?

- Can we see your line?

They will evaluate working with you based on your answers to these questions.

With our new way of getting sales reps, you will not have to pay that much or go through that much scrutiny. You simply want to go about finding interested candidates, as we mentioned above. Next, you will want to let them know that it is only a part-time job. The key words here are "part time job." If you are just starting, you really do not need a full time sales rep because you do not have enough merchandise to support it. If you do want to use them full time, be prepared to pay.

The benefits of part-time might include:

- They consider it just extra money;

- They can still keep their current job;

- You don't have to pay benefits;

- Part of their draw is guaranteed even if they don't get sales;

- Guaranteed draw doesn't have to be that much (couple of hundred a month);

- Commission should be excellent (around 8 to 13%);

- Draw increases with sales;

- Work in their own city and metropolitan area (no traveling beyond 50 to 75 miles).

Considerations of full-time include:

- They will want a larger guaranteed draw;
- Commission could be lower than if they were part-time since draw will be higher;
- They may or may not be willing to leave their current job;
- More than likely, they will want an advance at the beginning of the contract;
- Will work inside their metropolitan area;
- Will also have to travel outside of their metropolitan area;
- You will pick up travel expenses.

The choice is yours as to what employment status you want. Our plan was to use reps on part-time basis while utilizing them in their own city. We reasoned that they know where the retailers are in their city and can get to them easily. They can be more consistent in getting in touch with buyers who are sometimes hard to catch up with. In general, how you want to set up your contract between you and your reps is up to you. We will give you an example of one of our contracts at the back of this guide for your reference.

What you will require from your reps:

- Telephone with unlimited long distance;

- Email account;

- Fax Machine (optional);

- Printer;

- Software like Microsoft Excel, Word, and Graphic Software that prints pictures (You may be able to print files at somewhere like a Kinko's);

- Great customer service and sales skills;

- Fully knowledgeable about all about the products they will be selling from design details, fabrication, and fit;

- Be fully knowledgeable of all of your sales strategies;

- Be enthusiastic and take pride in selling your products;

- Formulate new ideas sometime to help in selling and getting new accounts; and

- Be willing to travel locally to various retailers (must have transportation).

You must be able to provide reps with:

- Business cards;

- Any catalogs, line sheets, and promotional items you have;

- Samples;

- Order sheets;

- Sales training;

- Full knowledge and background on your company; and

- Steps to take in setting up their sales services as a business. You will want your reps to act as **independent contractors** so you do not have to pay any taxes on them. It will be their responsibility to pay taxes and so on if you structure their positions this way. They will need to get a DBA similar to the way you did when you set up your clothing line.

Now we will go on to the sale training section. In general, our sales training can be used for yourself and for other reps.

Sales Rep Training Outline

Step 1: Retaining knowledge of all of your company's key points, background, and history;

Step 2: Taking in the samples and related information;

Step 3: Finding stores that meet your criteria;

Step 4: Making contact and getting appointments;

Step 5: Arriving at the appointment;

Step 6: The presentation;

Step 7: They want to write an order but may say or ask some of these things.

Step 8: After writing the order with them, do these things:

Step 9: Notifying us and follow-ups

Step 10: Other recommendations

Step 1: Your reps should know the following:

- When your line was started;
- Where the company is based;
- An understanding of how your clothes fit;
- Your niche;
- If any celebrities are wearing your line;
- The name of a comparable line;
- The type of store you sell to;
- Your price points;
- Whether you do the Magic or other tradeshows;

- Your plan for driving customers into your account's stores;
- Who your target customer is (demographics, trendsetter, trend follower, etc.);
- What category of clothing you are designing;
- Where your manufacturing is done;
- Where you advertise;
- Whether your garments come with price tags on them;
- Whether your orders are pre-packed or open stock;
- Your shipper (FedEx, UPS etc.);
- The cities in which you have retailers;
- Your sales goal for them and your company as a whole;
- Terms and conditions for your retailers;
- The type of stores you want them to approach;
- Your plans on distribution; and
- Your general size range.

Step 2: Your rep takes in your samples and related information:

1. You send out samples to the sales rep.
2. Rep receives them.
3. Rep should have a full understanding of your information sheets such as order forms and garment detail information.
4. Rep should have a one-color suitcase to keep and store all information and samples in.
5. On the day of the appointment, be sure to have suitcase with wrinkle-free garments inside.

6. Other things to have in their suitcase: a pen, business cards, calculator, several order forms, postcards, magazine that features the product.

7. Answer any of their questions.

Step 3: Finding stores that meet your criteria:

1. Find stores that carry similar brands or prices compatible to yours.

2. The store cannot sell any items that are knock-offs.

3. The store must not be a discount retailer unless this is your market.

4. The store must be well organized and not too cluttered.

5. The store must have an attractive store front if outside of a mall.

6. After you get the account, the next account should be at least three to four miles from that account (this is up to you, of course).

7. Allow rep to ask you any questions.

Step 4: Making contact – getting appointments:

1. Just showing up sometimes is good if you cannot get the right person on the phone or they will not commit to an appointment.

    A. Go in and talk with manager;

    B. Introduce yourself and let the manager know what company you represent;

    C. Show manager a couple of garments and related info. Leave postcards with them;

    D. Let them know that the buyer should definitely get in contact with you;

E. Ask them if they like your clothing;

F. This could lead to a meeting with the buyer.

2. When calling for the appointment:

A. Be very friendly and professional;

B. Script (you): Hello, I am _____ calling from _____ (your company). We are a ____ (your category and niche) clothing brand. I would very much like to come in and meet with you. I would like to do a very quick presentation that will not take up too much of your time. I promise you will not be disappointed. We have some great designs and low minimums.

C. (Then – they may say): I am not looking for any new lines right now.

D. (You Say): You should make an exception for our collection. We have very low minimums so it is easy for you to test our line out. It is important for us to make you money. We have a great fit and excellent quality on top of unique designs. We have a number of different promotions that we will be doing to bring traffic to our accounts. The number of people seeking new brands is increasing, as each person now wants to look different from the next person. You also will have exclusivity with our line in your area.

E. (Them - they may say): I have never heard of the line.

F. (You say) That is quite understandable as we are somewhat new to your area. We have been in ____ (any magazines, shows etc.)

3. Set up appointment and keep it. Arrive to the appointment on time.

4. If you do not get appointment, ask if you can call them later, if we still have openings in their area.

5. Follow up the next month.

Step 6: Arriving at the appointment:

- Arrive on time.

- Be sure you relax yourself. Do not be nervous.

- Be fully knowledgeable of this training course.

- Be sure to have organized wrinkle-free clothing in your suitcase.

- Be sure you have all necessary info.

- Arrive at the store and ask for the buyer.

- Introduce yourself and let them know what company you are with.

- When they come out, compliment them on their store and introduce yourself.

- Ask them where they want you to set up.

- Let them know you will not take up much of their time. "I know you are very busy. I appreciate you meeting with me."

- Give them your business card, or you can wait. Judge by the situation.

Step 7: Your Presentation:

- Give them some of the key points of your company.

- Let them know about your minimums.

- Pull out clothes matching items together as this top matches with this and so on.

- You may pull them out one at a time while the buyer is looking.

- Encourage them to feel the fabric and talk about how nice it is.
- Talk about the garment detailing:
    - The sizes it comes in;
    - The color of the garment;
    - How the garment fits;
    - The inseam if related to jeans;
    - How each item ties into everything else in the collection to give consumers a choice as to how they mix and match up the outfit.
- Do not mention price until you are finished with the presentation. If they ask, tell them.
- After showing all the garments and explaining them, present the owner/buyer with your line sheets.
- Give them the order sheet.
- Let them know the order sheet has the prices on it for them to look at.
- Let them know that they will have exclusivity with your product in their area because we do not sell to stores within a three to four mile radius of each other.
- You could also be wearing one of your pieces to help show the product off.
- You could also have a model or two with you to help show some of your pieces off.

Next, you will let them know and do the following:

- Let them know what styles you have in stock that are ready for immediate shipping and when the others will be shipped. Give them a **30-day delivery window** on not-in-stock items. For instance, if you plan to have xyz jeans on

January 1, you will want to tell them they will have **xyz** jeans between January 5 and February 5.

- Ask a customer or sale's clerk to give their opinion if they seem to be interested in what is going on. This can help you out in terms of getting the sale if others like your line.
- Let them fill out the order form. Be sure to get all contact info.
- Let them know your terms.
- Let them know that if anything is wrong with their order they can give you a call and that you will take care of them.

Step 8: They want to write an order but may say or ask some of these things:

- Concern over minimums. Strike a deal with them if you really want the account.
- If they do not do COD, let them know you will try to get them factored if you are factoring. If you are not, you will have to convince them to do COD.
- "I just want to do a trial order. If it works out, I will order more." You say: "That is fine."
- They say, "We have already spent our budget for this season." You say: "Is it possible for you to do a small test order with us? I would hate to see you pass up this opportunity to have exclusivity with our brand in your area. We have low minimums. Even if you just try out a few pieces. Let us make you some extra money."
- They say, "Ship half this date and half on this date." You say, "Not a problem."
- They ask for a discount. If you have some type of discount in place, such as a quantity discount, let them know.

- They ask, "Will you give me posters and other items that I can display?" Let them know if you will be sending them with their order.
- If they ask, "Are you doing any magazines?" Tell them what you are going to do.
- "Do you ship on time?" Tell them, "Yes, we do."
- They ask how you will market the product in their area or city. Tell them your plans.
- Let them keep one copy of the order sheet and line sheets. You keep the master color copies of line sheets and make exact duplicate copy of the order sheet.
- If they do not write an order after you have done all of the above, ask, once again, if they are sure they do not want to do a test order at very low risk to them. Ask them what if you let them order one outfit, just to see how their customers like it. Ask if you can follow up with them later if you still have an opening in their area.
- If they say no, do not feel bad. Some will take in a new line and some will not.
- After writing up an order, thank them for their business.

9: After writing the order with them, do these things:

- Give the store advice on how to market/sell your line (very important);
- Ask them can they let their employees get a little familiar with your line;
- When selling, they should let customers know about your niche in the market;
- Let the customers know about any other highlights of your brand such as magazines you are in;
- Encourage their customers to try your clothing on to see how great your fit is.

Next, you end everything by:

- Folding the clothing up and placing them back into the suitcase;
- Gather all of the order sheets and all the things you must keep;
- Shake their hand and thank them for their business;
- Once again, let them know that the sales manager will call them to verify the order;
- Let them know you will see them in two to four weeks, as soon as the next items come out;
- Answer any questions they may have. If they ask anything you do not know, do not hesitate to say, "excuse me," and then walk to the side to call someone from your cell phone who has the answer.

Step 10: Rep notifying you and follow ups:

- Reps should call you to let you know how the appointment went;
- Rep should fax in order on the same day that it was written;
- You verify the order that day or the next day;
- Ship the order out without delay after verification;
- When you ship the order to that store, let the rep know when exactly the store accepted the merchandise. Use the tracking number to get this information.
- You follow up with a thank you call and make sure everything is okay with their order.

Step 11: Other recommendations

- Practice your full presentation on family members and friends prior to going out in the field.

- Practice filling out the order sheet and calculating totals.

- All of your reps should be passing out postcards when they can.

Department Stores and Large Chains

It is a little trickier to get your line into large chains; however, it can be done. First, you will want to follow portions of the sales training guide that applies. You will make contact the same way. Department stores and chains may want to know these things, in addition to having other provisions for you:

- How the line will be packed;
- The type of hangers to use in some cases;
- The barcode information;
- Where to ship the order;
- When they want you to ship the order;
- Discounting if the product doesn't sell well;
- Returns if the product doesn't sell well;
- They will be big on your advertising/marketing plan;
- Verifying that you ship on time;
- Your line for quality assurance;
- They will negotiate for better price points.

Getting in a department store is hard work. Staying in a department store is even harder. Once you are out of a department store, it is very hard to get back in. Be sure before you approach department stores your company is running smoothly and shipping on time. Do not just rush into a department store deal if it falls in your lap; you may never get another chance if it goes wrong the first time. Develop your line a little more first, working out quality, pricing, and shipping issues. This is our advice.

Shipping

Shipping is a very important part of keeping your accounts alive. You should show great attention to shipping. You will want to make sure your orders are packed correctly. You will want to make sure that all pricing and styles ordered are correct. If you are sending COD, you want to make sure the COD label is correct. In general, do not try to make money on shipping. Charge your accounts what the shipment will cost + $1 or $2 for packaging materials.

Be sure to keep up with tracking numbers once the order is shipped. Retailers will often call you asking for tracking numbers and when their package will be arriving. It is a good idea to have additional insurance on the package over the $100 that most carriers give you automatically.

Closing Advice

In closing, we would like to wish you the best of luck in selling your brand to retailers. We hope this guide has been beneficial to you in terms of understanding how to deal with retailers. Retailers are the lifeline of your company. Without them, you will find it hard to make it. It is best that you offer the best customer service that you can. You should seek to build relationships.

You should remember that your job of helping the retailer sell your merchandise never stops. You must make it a point to stay in contact with your retailers at least every two weeks to check on them. If your products are selling, retailers will keep ordering. The goal is to build with each store becoming a solid rock. Good Luck and God Bless!

(On the Next Page is a sample line sheet for your reference. Do not copy designs seen on line sheet!)

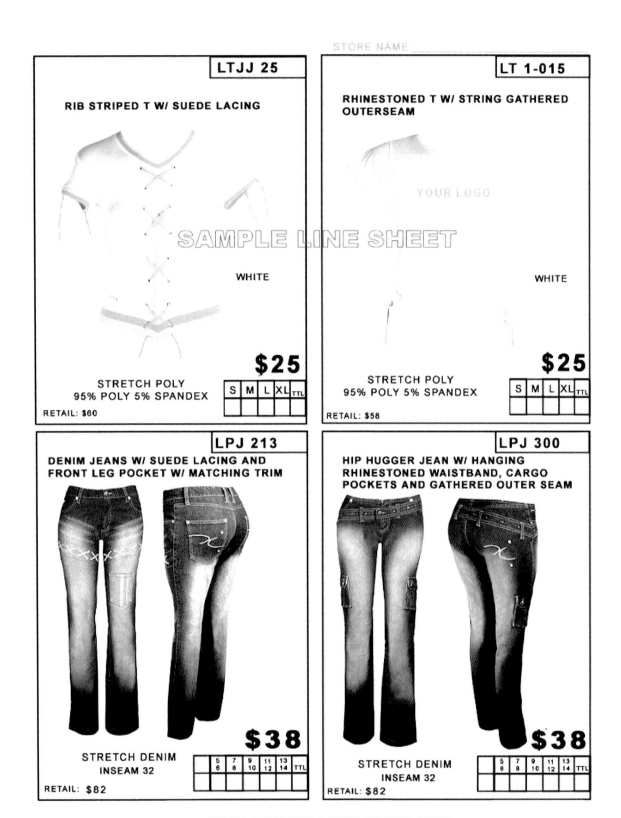

LTJJ 25

RIB STRIPED T W/ SUEDE LACING

WHITE

$25

STRETCH POLY
95% POLY 5% SPANDEX

S	M	L	XL	TTL

RETAIL: $60

LT 1-015

RHINESTONED T W/ STRING GATHERED
OUTERSEAM

YOUR LOGO

SAMPLE LINE SHEET

WHITE

$25

STRETCH POLY
95% POLY 5% SPANDEX

S	M	L	XL	TTL

RETAIL: $58

LPJ 213

DENIM JEANS W/ SUEDE LACING AND
FRONT LEG POCKET W/ MATCHING TRIM

$38

STRETCH DENIM
INSEAM 32

5 6	7 8	9 10	11 12	13 14	TTL

RETAIL: $82

LPJ 300

HIP HUGGER JEAN W/ HANGING
RHINESTONED WAISTBAND, CARGO
POCKETS AND GATHERED OUTER SEAM

$38

STRETCH DENIM
INSEAM 32

5 6	7 8	9 10	11 12	13 14	TTL

RETAIL: $82

YOUR COMPANY CONTACT INFO HERE

(Below is a sample order sheet for your reference.)

Your Company Name
Your Company Contact Information

ORDER TOTAL:	
STORE NAME:	
SALESPERSON	
INVOICE DATE	
ORDER DATE:	
TERMS	

ORDER INFO:

Style #	Color	S	M	L	XL	2XL	TOTAL		
								$30	$0.00
		ONE SIZE							
								$15	$0.00
		2	4	6	8	10			
								$40	$0.00
		30	32	34	36	40			
								$40	$0.00

SHIP TO:

TOTAL:	$0.00
SHIPPING:	
DISCOUNTS:	
TOTAL:	$0.00

PLEASE MAKE PAYMENTS TO:
Your Company
MONEY ORDER OR CASH - NO CHECKS!

Get spec sheet templates, contracts, purchase order forms & more with The Fashion

Business Center at StartingaClothingLine.com

Your Company Here

PART-TIME – Sales Rep / Independent Contractor

Agreement

PURPOSE: The purpose of this contract is an agreement between (your company) and (sales rep and his/or company name) Rep is acting as an independent contractor.

Goals: It is our objective to increase our sales in various territories effective immediately.

Overall Compensation Plan: Commission and Draw.

Part-Time Position: This is a part-time position, which is the determining factor of amount of draw and commission offered. You more than likely will spend an average time of 10- 20 hours per week on our program.

Before Officially Starting: Sales Rep must furnish by fax, mail, or email a copy of State Drivers License.

Official Start Date: Official start date will be once rep is furnished with samples / materials to begin the selling process.

Terms:

1. Commission:

   A. 10% of unit wholesale cost (does not include shipping charges accessed on invoices)

   B. Paid weekly once payments from accounts clear your company bank account.

   C. Commission on rep's accounts only.

   D. Funds from each sale must clear bank prior to payment being made on each particular invoice – this could delay payment as banks typically have a 5-day hold.

   When and if rep no longer works for your company for any reason: Commission policy:

   A. If rep no longer works for company under any circumstances, he/she will be paid commission on rep's accounts for 4 months following ending of this contract, providing the accounts in question are still active buyers with (your company).

2. **Draw Details and Objectives**

   A. Draw of $150 per week will begin 30 days after your official start date providing you are selling $4,000 and above per month.

B. Draw Schedule: Biweekly – Paid on the 1st and 15th of each month. $300 every two weeks.

C. If your sales are between $2,000 and $4,000 per month you will only receive $250 per month draw payment paid out on the 1st of the month.

D. If your sales are below $2,000 you are ineligible for draw payments and you will receive only commissions on your sales.

E. Why should you continue if your sales are less than $2,000 per month? Because things could turn around in your area at any time and you will be in position to take advantage of it when it does.

3. **Bonuses** (Totally Optional – You decide on this)

   A. Bonuses will begin during month 4 after 90-day trial period.
      a. Bi-weekly sales / shipped / and paid by retailer of $5,000 will yield a $250 bonus.
      b. Bi-weekly sales / shipped / and paid for by retailer of $10,000 + will yield a $500 Bonus.
   B. If for any reason a retailer cancels an order or fails to pay for it when it reaches them, their order will not count towards meeting sales goal for that bi-weekly period.

4. **Taxes / Records:**
   A. All commission and profit sharing points will be documented.
   B. All expenditures must be documented.
   C. Rep will receive quarterly company financial statements.

D. Rep will be its own separate company from your company. Rep will act as an independent contractor.

E. Rep must report their earnings to government entities and pay taxes as a business.

5. Trial Period:

A. Initial 30-day trial period to see how you perform within the first 30 days.

B. Full - Trial Period last for 3 months (90 days) from official start date.

C. Either party can end contract with just cause if issues cannot be resolved.

6. Sales Rep's Responsibilities:

A. Provide excellent customer service on serviced accounts.

B. Obtain new accounts that meet your company's criteria.

C. Lead generation and follow your company's leads when applicable.

D. Fully Legible orders

E. Represent company in professional manner.

F. Meet sales objectives for opening new accounts.

G. Keep positive attitude and work ethic.

H. Excellent team player skills

I. Keep samples in good condition.

J. Lost or destroyed samples must be paid for by Rep at wholesale cost

K. Report / Fax in orders no later than day after they were made.

L. Stop selling a product once you are informed it is sold out.

M. When displaying clothes make sure they look neat and unwrinkled

N. Be fully knowledgeable about garments when you are selling (we will help)

O. Return samples to your company if requested to do so

P. Check with your accounts once every two weeks to see how product is doing

Q. Report all feedback from Retailers and consumers regarding our products

7. (Your Company's) Responsibilities:

A. Help you in any problems you may be facing during the selling process and in appt. scheduling

B. Provide excellent customer service to your accounts

C. On call at anytime for any questions and problem solving

D. Help out with leads in your area when we can

E. Ship on time

F. Verify orders prior to ship

G. Accurate accounting of commissions

H. Operate in respectable manner.

I. Provide samples, catalogs and other items needed to make sales.

8. Professionalism:

A. You agree to represent (your company name) in the best possible manner

B. You agree not to commit any fraud or ill will at any time while representing our company.

C. You agree to be honest with buyers and retailers to the best of your knowledge.

D. You agree to accurately write up orders.

E. You agree to show respect and the utmost courtesy when in the company of retailers.

F. You agree to dress appropriately for each sales meeting and be on time.

9. Confidentiality

A. Sale Rep can in no way say anything negative about any aspect of our company to any persons or entities that may conflict with our image.

B. Rep may not seek to damage our standing with any clients should rep for any reason depart with (Your company name here)

C. (Your company) will have the right to seek damages in the court of law should this agreement on confidentially be broken.

By signing this contract, you are stating that you understand and agree to all the terms and conditions listed in the (your company name here) / Independent Sales Contractor agreement:

Full Name:_____

Full Address:_____

Home Phone:_____ Cell Phone:_____

Email Address:_____

I enter and agree to all of the terms and conditions set fourth in this sales rep contract between me and (your company name here). My signature is proof of my consent.

Signature of Sales Rep:_____

Notary info below: This agreement must be notarized.

Note: Please initial each page and sign this page.

Special Notice:

Get spec sheet templates, contracts, purchase order forms & more with The Fashion Business Center at StartingaClothingLine.com